HOW TO (FISH EVERY TIME

YOUR SUCCESS GUIDE
TO THE GREAT LAKES
AND TRIBUTARIES

A comprehensive success manual for catching

more fresh and saltwater species. Written for

fishermen by a fisherman:

Capt. Michael Peel

GPI

Global Publishing, Inc.

Walled Lake, Michigan

Additional copies of this book may be ordered through bookstores or by sending $12.95 plus $3.50 for postage and handling to:
Publishers Distribution Service
6893 Sullivan Road
Grawn, MI 49637
(800) 345-0096

Illustrations and cover design by Global Publishing, Inc.
Cover art by Erich Carlson

Publisher's Cataloging-in-Publication Data

Peel, Michael, 1953-
        How to catch more fish every time : your success guide to the Great Lakes and tributaries : a comprehensive success manual for catching more fresh and saltwater species : written for fishermen / by a fisherman, Michael Peel -- Walled Lake, MI : Global Publishing., c1994.
        p. : ill. ; cm.

        Includes bibliographical references and index.
        ISBN: 0-9640301-0-1
        1. Fishing--Great Lakes Region. I. Title

SH464.G8P44   1994
799.12'0977 dc20   94-075228
Manufactured in the United States of America and distributed worldwide.

* DEDICATION *

This book is written in loving memory of my father Robert Charles Peel who was truly one of the greatest sportsmen and sailors that I ever knew.

CONTENTS

ACKNOWLEDGMENT

Special thanks to Dennis M. Ende of Holland, Michigan who gave me some valuable information on early spring pier and surf fishing. He is a very proficient and knowledgeable fisherman who has had many outstanding catches from the surf and piers.

Thanks to Bill Bale from Saugatuck, Michigan for his input on electronics explained in this book. Besides being a good friend, Bill is an expert on electronic fishing equipment and its proper installation.

A BRIEF FORWARD

This book will drastically improve your fishing success for salmon, trout, walleye, and perch anywhere in the Great Lakes whether you fish from a small boat, large boat, from a pier, or in the surf. Using tips and techniques I have learned in twenty-five years of charter fishing, I will explain and guide you through many different circumstances that will help you consistently catch more fish.

We will be starting out in the early spring fishing for brown trout, coho, and king salmon. Then I will take you offshore as the in-shore water warms up and teach you the secrets of catching big lake trout, steelhead, and salmon near the surface as they feed on schools of bait fish. As the season progresses, I'll explain downrigger patterns and many techniques to catch fish when they go deep. There will also be an entire chapter on open water perch fishing that will enable you to catch them by the hundreds. How and where to catch walleye in rivers, bays, and open water will be explained in depth. You will learn techniques that will enable you to take these very popular game fish from spring through fall. Then, as the water cools, I'll cover fall fishing for both spawning salmon and steelhead. Other tips that will be covered are boat handling, landing and cleaning fish, great fish recipes, and rigging your boat to make it a "fishing machine."

Even though this book is written primarily about fishing for salmon, trout, walleye, and perch in the Great Lakes, all of the described techniques and information will work for many species of saltwater fish throughout the world. Information in this book will be valuable to all fishermen pursuing striped bass, walleye, salmon, trout, and many other species that are stocked in reservoirs, rivers, and lakes across North America.

So, read on and be prepared to double your catch this season. And, remember to proceed with caution. You should always be aware of water conditions and never take chances in and around the water. Every year anglers die as a result of foolishness and/or carelessness on their own part or on the part of others.

CHAPTER *1*

EARLY SPRING FISHING

As soon as the ice breaks up on the Great Lakes, the fishing action for salmon and brown trout begins to get hot. The first places to seek good action are warm water discharges at power plants and harbor mouths, where the desired warmer water empties into the lake. First, I will talk about fishing at river mouths that attract feeding salmon and trout.

Spring Pier Head Fishing

Most of the rivers that enter into the Great Lakes have pier heads, which are excellent platforms to fish from. Pier heads provide an excellent structure to fish from because they typically protrude far out into the lake. They also offer superior cover and habitat for fish. Many bait fish will find sanctuary around their wooden pilings or rocky foundations. This, in turn, attracts game fish who

1

feed on the bait present and also seek the security of this manmade cover. Since the river water warms before the lake water, the best spot to fish is in the river itself between the pier heads. The game fish come into this water because it's warmer, and to feed on the bait that is naturally attracted to the warm water, or is being washed downstream by strong spring currents. After the warming water has an effect on the lake water around the piers, the fishing will be good on the lake side of the piers also.

Dennis Ende with a four-man limit of brown trout caught while pier fishing with spawn in the early spring.

Because the early spring water is very cold making the fish less aggressive, most of them will be caught on spawn or bait while still fishing. They simply don't have the energy to chase down and strike a lure. Spawn is usually used in two ways -- either fished in spawn sacks or chunk spawn. Spawn sacks are five to ten individual salmon or steelhead eggs placed in fine nylon netting and tied into a small cluster. If you don't have your own eggs to make them, pre-tied spawn sacks can be purchased from many sporting goods stores. The best color for the nylon netting (that is available in many colors) is generally orange. However, some fishermen do use chartreuse when fishing in dark or murky water. Orange colored netting is the most consistent producer because it assimilates the same natural color of salmon and trout spawn.

A good choice of rods for fishing spawn are eight to nine foot light action graphite rods with a cork handle. Using a cork handle rod will enable you to feel a strike much better than with a foam handle, because the strike is transmitted through the rod into your hand much more effectively. Any good medium size spinning reel should do the job. It should be loaded with six to eight pound test and have a large enough line capacity to handle a big fish. As far as line goes, any good quality monofilament, with the exclusion of florescent line, will work. Florescent lines are great for bass fishing, but I feel that they have the tendency to spook salmon and trout.

The best hooks for fishing spawn sacks would be a salmon egg hook size eight through four with a slice shank that holds the sack on the hook and a turned up eye for better hook ups on fish. Hide the hook in the spawn sack between the eggs so the fish won't detect it when they pick up the bait. When fishing chunk spawn I would recommend using a small treble (size ten or twelve) and tying the spawn onto the hook with a piece of light thread. This will keep light strikes from tearing the spawn off your hook, and keep it on the hook much better when casting.

The rigging for spawn fishing is very simple. Thread a snap swivel on the main line then tie a barrel swivel below it. Onto your barrel swivel tie your leader, which should be four to six feet long and made of four to eight pound test monofilament. If the water is clear or the current is light, use a light leader. When the water is murky or the current is strong, go with a heavier leader. The fish can't see your leader in murky water anyway and when the current is strong, you'll be able to hold instead of breaking off the big ones (See Figure 1.1).

An option to this simple rig just mentioned, is to add four or five BB size floats inside your spawn sack for buoyancy. These floats are made of styrofoam and commercially produced in a variety of colors. This very innovative method of rigging will cause the bait to float up resulting in more strikes from fish not swimming tight to the bottom. The desired height of the bait off the bottom can be controlled by adding a couple of split shot to the leader above the hook. Example -- with the split shot six inches above the hook, the bait will be approximately six inches off the bottom.

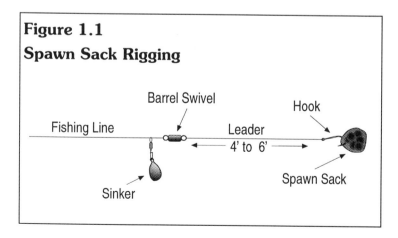

Figure 1.1
Spawn Sack Rigging

Other baits that will produce fish, especially later in the spring, are live alewife or dead smelt. Use these with the first rig mentioned, but use a larger treble hook (size 6 to 2). Alewife and smelt are especially effective when spawning bait fish move into the area that you are fishing.

For a sinker, use as heavy of one as necessary to hold your bait in position without drifting in the current. It's important to use a pyramid or flat sinker so it doesn't roll in the current and end up against the bank or pier head. This brings us back to the reason we use a snap swivel on our main line. The snap swivel allows us to change weights as we need them without re-rigging by hooking the sinker on the rig with the snap. Since it is threaded onto the main line, when a fish hits, the line will be pulled through the swivel allowing it to pick up the bait without feeling the weight. When you feel or see a strike, it is best to lower the rod slightly letting the fish take the bait then when you feel him again, set the hook. Using this technique, many fish are hooked deep in the mouth giving you a much better chance of landing them. For landing most fish from pier heads, it is very important to have a long handled dip net. I have seen many fishermen risking life and limb hanging over the cold water by one arm trying to reach fish with a short handled net.

When the water temperature reaches the low forties, another productive way to take salmon and trout from pier heads at river mouths is by casting with spoons. The best spoons for this type of fishing are ones that are fairly heavy so you can cast a considerable distance even in the wind. My favorite choice of spoons would be "Little Cleos" in colors blue and silver, chartreuse and silver, gold and red, and pearl with a red tip and the Luhr Jensen #3 "Loco Spoon" in gold with gold prism, white with silver prism, chartreuse with silver prism, and chrome blue with silver prism. Another good spoon is a "K.O. Wobbler" in gold with an orange stripe. When casting these spoons for salmon and trout if a steady retrieve isn't producing fish, another method that can be used is to cast out and allow the spoon to settle to bottom, retrieve halfway in, let it settle to bottom again, and finish your retrieve. Many times this will draw strikes from fish laying closer to the bottom.

Spring Surf Fishing

Surf fishing, or fishing from the beach, is another popular way to take fish in the early spring. When fishing with spawn in the surf, I would use the same techniques as described in river mouth fishing. It's very important in surf fishing to use a pyramid sinker because when you tighten your line to detect strikes, flat sinkers will want to slide towards the beach, whereas a pyramid sinker will dig in keeping your bait out away from the shore. With chest waders you can get out a little further and catch fish casting with the same spoons used for river mouth fishing.

There are two additional pieces of equipment that should be used for this type of fishing. One is a rod holder that can be stuck in the sand. You can buy rod holders like this, or make one yourself out of a piece of PVC pipe with a stake attached to it or cut on a sharp angle and driven into the sand. This is very important because it will keep your reel out of the sand and your rod tip high where a strike can be detected more easily. You will also need a pair of chest high insulated waders. For your safety I would strongly recommend you wear a life jacket or flotation vest while wading in the surf.

Warm Water Discharges

Fishing warm water discharges from power plants that are scattered around the Great Lakes provides some anglers with outstanding catches. You would use the same techniques as fishing river mouths or the surf when working these manmade fish attracters. At power plants where you can get a small boat to the water, trolling works great too. The same trolling methods that will be discussed next will work at warm water discharges.

Before I begin our discussion about trolling which will comprise much of this book, let me share two very important tips that should be used for any type of fishing. Number one -- sharp hooks catch fish! Very few hooks come sharp enough for use from the manufacturer. Use a file or a battery operated sharpener to make your hooks so sharp they won't slide across your thumbnail without sticking. The practice of using sharp hooks is the number one key in turning strikes into hooked fish. Number two --

keep your lures and equipment odor free. Gasoline, sunscreen, insect repellent, and many other odors will spook fish. Either they won't hit at all, or they will strike short making them hard to hook. I have seen many charter excursions that started out great go sour when the sunscreen comes out. Remember, a fish can smell foreign unnatural odors many times better than humans. Always have a bar of unscented Ivory soap in your tackle box and wash your hands before you start fishing. Preceding any fishing trip, use liquid Ivory soap to wash all your rods, reels, downrigger weights, and other tackle or lures that might have become contaminated from previous use. This procedure might sound troublesome, however it takes very little time and bears great rewards.

As the Water Warms

As the season progresses and the water temperature warms into the forties, fish will chase a spoon or body bait, and trolling will become the most consistent method of catching salmon and trout. Most fish will be caught either working river mouths or along the beach between the sand bars. When trolling river mouths, many fish are caught on the break where the river and lake water meet. This is a place that will concentrate fish as they're drawn to both warm water and an abundance of bait. Pay close attention when working this area as to whether the fish hit on the lake or the river water side of the break. Many days the fish will be laying right where the two waters meet and others primarily in the darker river water. One spot that proves to be particularly productive is where the break turns and heads towards the river. On that corner, many of your fish will be caught.

Another location that is particularly good for early spring fishing is trolling in between the sand bars along the beach. This is done by fishing parallel to the shoreline. Pay attention to your depth sounder as to where you are in relationship to the bars. In most lakes there is usually a series of three sand bars. Most fish are caught between the second and third bar. After a strike, try to remember where you were when the fish hit. Many times they will be on the outside slope of the second sand bar, dead in the middle of the hole between the sand bars, or on the inside slope of the third sand bar. This is very important! In an offshore wind, the fish will usually be laying on the outside slope of the second sand bar. It will be just the opposite during an on-shore wind positioning the fish either in the hole or on the inside slope of the outside bar. For boats without depth sounders, a downrigger weight near the bottom will tell you when you're starting to come up on one of the bars. Even with all the equipment on my boat, I use this technique very often. By turning in or out of the hole until your downrigger weights start bumping on the bottom then turning back towards the hole, you will be able to tell what slope of the sand bar you are fishing. Very often a strike will occur just as your weights stop bumping the bottom because the fish like the presentation of a bait coming down the slope of the bar into the hole.

Many types of equipment can be used both when fishing the break and between the bars. However, planer boards with body baits prove to be effective most often. Planer boards enable you to run multiple lures out to the side of the boat and let you present lures to the fish in shallow water without them being spooked by the boat. There are many good commercial planer boards on the market. Most of them now are offset double boards where the outside board is set slightly ahead of the inside board. This allows them both to catch water so there will be more resistance and they will pull farther out to the side of the boat. This design helps keep them out of your way while fighting and landing fish. It's best to have a bow mounted planer board mast equipped with reels on your boat. The mast will hold the tow lines up in the air and produce an angle in the towline so the fishing line releases will slide down to the boards much easier. The reels retain the tow-line allowing you to let out the boards the desired distance for use and retrieve them when you're finished fishing.

As with most fishing equipment available, there are many different types of planer boards, reels and masts on the market. They range from electric reels, manual reels, to homemade masts with no reels at all. Now, for fishing planer boards, you will need a release to attach your fishing lines to the tow line of the board. The releases that I use and recommend are the Wille "Deep Dive Tow Line Release" and the Laurvick "Visa-Grip Release." You will also need two or three rod holders on each side of the boat. They should be positioned so your rods can be set in a fan with the rod tips slightly vertically apart from each other.

To set the planer boards, put them out to the side of the boat from one hundred to one hundred and fifty feet then let your lure back anywhere from seventy-five to one hundred and fifty feet behind the boat. Then attach your line to the planer board release, then attach the release to the tow line that runs out to the board. Let line off the fishing reel until the first planer board release comes within two or three feet of the board. Then set the proper drag tension on the reel and place the rod in the rod holder closest to the bow of the boat. Repeat the process with the next rod by letting the lure out the same distance as the first one, hooking it to the planer board release, and letting it out two

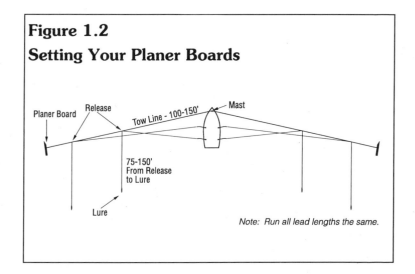

Figure 1.2
Setting Your Planer Boards

Planer Board | Release | Tow Line - 100-150' | Mast

75-150'
From Release
to Lure

Lure

Note: Run all lead lengths the same.

thirds of the way to the board. If a third rod is desired, repeat the process and let it out one third of the way to the planer board. With all the lures out the same distance behind the boat, you might think when a fish hits it will become tangled in the other lines. It usually won't because the distance between the end of the rod and the planer board release adds line when the fish strikes pulling it free from the release. This added line makes the rod that has been pulled free farther back behind the boat than the other ones, clearing all the other lines automatically (See Figure 1.2).

Fishing Flat Lines and Downriggers Together

Flat lines run directly behind the boat with body baits, and sometimes spoons, will take fish too. Small boats without planer boards will often take many fish on flat lines because they don't spook fish as easily in shallow water as larger boats do. I usually run my flat lines between one hundred and ten and one hundred and thirty feet behind the boat. Even though flat lines and planer boards produce a lot of your catch in the early spring, don't count out downriggers. I've seen days where spoons on my downriggers have outproduced the body baits on planer boards and flat lines. When fishing downriggers in shallow water it's best to keep your outside long arm downriggers (outdowns) shallower than the ones on the stern of the boat. The reason for this is they have less of a tendency to spook fish because the boat doesn't have to run directly over them before they get to the lure. Many times we'll catch king salmon, coho salmon, and brown trout only four to five feet down with a lure twenty to thirty feet behind the downrigger weight. I usually start out with my downriggers only this far back and then if they don't go and I'm having action on my planer boards and flat lines, I will drop them back accordingly. Be careful not to put them too far back or you'll end up with fish off your high lines getting tangled in your downriggers. It can make quite a mess!

My best body baits for planer board and flat line fishing are Storm "Deep Junior ThunderStick" in metallic blue herringbone, metallic gold-orange back, pearl, and fire tiger. Storm 1/4 and 1/2 ounce "Hot-N-Tots", and 3/8 ounce "RattleTots" in metallic blue herringbone, florescent green herringbone, chartreuse, metallic gold-black back, and fire tiger, the Heddon 1/2 ounce "Tadpolly" in silver, blue and silver, and florescent red-black dots. I also use minnow style body baits like Bomber "Long-A's" in florescent green-pearl belly, florescent red, and blue and silver.

For body baits to fish to their full potential they must be running properly. If they are running off to one side or don't want to stay in the water, they should be "tuned." Most body baits have a wire eye that has a split ring where you attach your line to the lure. With needle nose pliers, bend the wire eye slightly the opposite direction the lure is running off to the side of the boat and experiment until the lure is running true. For lures like a "Hot-N-Tot" that have a metal lip and a connecting link, the proper procedure to tune is to bend the connecting link at the mid-joint where the clasp is located. This can be done with your bare hands and does not usually require needle nose pliers. If the lure is running to the right, place the end of your thumb on the clasp and your index finger on the top of the connecting link. Bend the top of the connecting link slightly to the left for lures running to the right. Do just the opposite for lures running to the left, and experiment until the lure is running true. My best producing "Hot-N-Tots" are ones that rock from side to side when being trolled or retrieved. Remember, when tuning all body baits never bend or twist the lip (bill) itself. This will cause permanent damage making the lure useless. Occasionally you will buy a lure that cannot be tuned. This is usually because of a misaligned lip or another manufacturer's defect. In this event, if you send it back to the manufacturer or dealer it will usually be replaced free of charge.

My favorite spoons for early spring fishing are Magna-Dyne standard size "Northport Nailers" in colors black-red prism tape, white-orange vinyl tape with white scallops, chartreuse-orange vinyl tape with chartreuse scallops, and silver-blue prism tape with dark blue-prism scallops. Lake Products #3 "Charger" in chartreuse with orange dots, white with florescent red dots, and florescent red-white V. The Luhr Jensen #3 "Loco" in gold-gold prism tape, blue-silver prism tape, and florescent red-silver prism tape. I also do very well on the Wolverine Tackle Company's 1/2 ounce "Silver Streak" in hammered silver-laser blue tape, blue prism scallops, and gold-gold prism tape.

For knowing what color of lure to use on a certain day -- I generally use silver baits or combinations of silver and color on bright days, and gold, or dark colored lures during overcast and low light conditions. Many different size lures produce fish during this time of the year. One thing you must keep in mind; when fish are feeding on spawning smelt, long thin baits such as the "Silver Streaks," "Junior ThunderSticks," and "Bombers" seem to outproduce the other lures.

Early spring fishing is available to sportsmen with or without boats. Even though optimum water temperatures for all species are far below their preferred zones, most fish will seek the warmest water available causing them to concentrate and feed in these areas. During cold water conditions, a slower troll or presentation of your bait will usually result in more fish. These spring cold water conditions offer small boat fishermen opportunities to have catches equal to or better than that of fishermen with large boats. There are two major reasons for this. One is the ability of smaller boats to work tighter trolling patterns thus allowing them to stay in more productive waters. The other is in shallow water during heavy boat traffic or sunny days, small boats have less of a tendency to spook fish. Take advantage of this super time to fish that is available in all of the Great Lakes.

CHAPTER *2*

OFFSHORE SPRING FISHING FOR KINGS, LAKERS AND STEELHEAD

Offshore spring fishing can offer some of the hottest action of the year for all species of salmon and trout, except for brown trout. Catching big lake trout, steelhead, coho, and king salmon near the surface makes this a very popular time to fish for trollers with all sizes of boats. This fishing usually takes place during May and June where beautiful spring weather enables smaller boats to venture further offshore with relative safety. If you are a small boat fisherman, I would strongly suggest that you have a VHF radio and flares on board, in case your boat becomes disabled. There are many good hand held VHF radios on the market that are very affordable and have weather channels built right into them. If you do become disabled because of mechanical problems, the water might be too deep for you to anchor and without some way to get assistance, you could drift anywhere. This is also true for larger boats, however, most of them are already equipped with radios. Besides for safety, a radio will let you hear how the other boats are doing. This will permit you to make the proper adjustments on depth, methods of fishing, and colors of baits that are producing for other boats. When fishing in unknown waters, it never hurts to ask at the local tackle or sports shop what channel the fishermen & charter boats communicate on. The airwaves belong to everybody, so feel free to eavesdrop on the action.

Finding the Fish

To find productive waters to fish, I look for a drop in the surface water temperature of two degrees or more when running out, or schools of bait fish and game fish. Surface temperature breaks can be found with a surface temperature gauge or visually, by looking for a change in water color or a line of debris and floating insects. Both are good indicators of a dominant temperature change. A debris or insect line is often referred to as a "scum line." The phrase "scum line" might sound a little nasty, but I know of nothing else that concentrates fish more when they are in the top forty feet. The best way I've found to work them is to "zigzag" troll through the break, paying attention to what side the fish hit on. If the fish are inside the break, you might want to concentrate your fishing effort in that area doing the same when they're outside of it. During this time of year, the fish will be feeding on both bait fish and insects which will congregate in this area attracting all species. If you are targeting steelhead, there's no better place to fish than an area with a sharp break in surface temperature or a scum line. When fishing a scum line, you should note that the stomach contents of all the steelhead you catch, and many of the lake trout, will contain mostly insects. These insects are usually comprised of flying species such as flies and moths or water beetles.

Another excellent place to fish is an area that holds schools of bait fish that are suspended or just under the surface. If you find such an area and you have a Loran or plotter, store it's location immediately. Smaller boats without Lorans or plotters can mark this location by throwing out a buoy. Most often you will find the game fish just downwind or down current from these schools of bait. With your fish finder you might also see the game fish laying just below them. When working an area like this that holds schools of bait and game fish, I prefer to work the edges of this spot. The reason for this is, in clear water if you troll directly through these schools, you will often spook and disburse them.

When fishing in South Florida, I learned the importance of watching for seabirds feeding on the ocean to locate fish. Many freshwater fishermen ignore this event that could lead them to schools of bait and actively feeding game fish. The birds might be attracted by bait fish just under the surface, or crippled bait that may have been wounded by actively feeding game fish. Keep in mind when trolling in a large body of open water, fish aren't everywhere. Try to find something that concentrates them. This will greatly improve your success.

Just like when fishing river mouths, warm water discharges at power plants, and along the beach, planer boards and flat lines will produce many of your fish when they're hitting near the surface. For the proper way to fish your boards, use the same techniques explained in Chapter

1. The best rods to use on your boards and flat lines should have a light or medium action, and be from seven to eight feet in length. Reels should have a high enough gear ratio to pick up line quickly and a large enough line capacity to handle big fish. My favorite reel to use is the Diawa SG 27 LC Line Counter reel. This level wind reel is large enough to have a good line capacity, but not too awkward or clumsy to use. It has a great handle, and is very fast when having a fish charge the boat or for getting lines out of the way. The line counter readout on the top of the reel tells you exactly how much line you have out.

If you don't have line counter reels, there are two ways you can estimate the amount of line you have out. One is to "pull" the line off the reel in approximately two feet increments. Whereas fifty "pulls" would equal one hundred feet of line or sixty "pulls" -- one hundred and twenty feet of line. The other method is to count the number of times the level wind goes across the reel. There will be a different amount of line out for each path of the level wind on various brands of reels. To determine how much line you have out on your reel, let it out one pass of the level wind then measure it and judge accordingly.

For line on your reel I would recommend a good low stretch monofilament in twelve to fifteen pound test. I prefer a line with a light pigment (color) to it either in blue, green, or pink. The reason light pigmented line works better in clear water where there is a lot of light present, is because of its ability to diffuse light. Clear line may allow sunlight to shine through it causing a prism effect or a reflection problem caused by its shiny coating.

In-Line Devices

Another device that will enable you to present baits to spooky fish near the surface is an in-line planer board. In-line planers are small boards that attach directly to your fishing line itself with a release system. When the line is hooked to the release, the in-line planer will run out to the side of the boat with the lure trailing behind it. After a strike, the release breaks free from the front of the board then the board turns around and slides back towards the fish. To keep the board from sliding all the way down to the bait, I tie on a split ring or large swivel for a stop and then use a leader about one rod length long. Without this split ring to stop your board, it will slide all the way down to the bait or the fish you're fighting. This will result in it slapping against the fish causing it to panic or become tangled in the lure which will damage it, or cause it to be pulled out of the fish's mouth. If you want your lure to run deeper, use a rubber core sinker from one half to two ounces in weight placing it between the split ring or swivel and the in-line planer board. Instead of rubber core sinkers, some fishermen prefer bullet shaped slip sinkers that are stopped from sliding down against the lure by the split ring or swivel. When a fish is hooked and fighting, they feel that the slip sinker will then have a negative effect on losing the fish. This is because the fishing line can slide through the sinker when the fish pulls hard, jumps, or makes a fast run.

To set your in-line boards, let your lure back fifty to one hundred feet behind the boat. Attach the back of the board to your fishing line first, and then to the release on the front of the board. Let the board out the desired distance to the side of the boat, setting the proper drag tension and placing it in a rod holder. You may run two or three boards on each side of the boat when spaced properly. It is

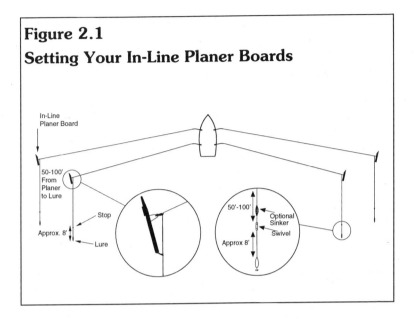

Figure 2.1
Setting Your In-Line Planer Boards

In-Line
Planer Board

50-100'
From
Planer
to Lure

Stop

Approx. 8'

Lure

50'-100'
Optional
Sinker
Swivel

Approx 8'

important to place the rod that has the board farthest out from the boat in the rod holder towards the bow, and the rod with the board closest to the boat in the holder towards the stern. When a fish hits the outside rod, there will be more line out which will enable it to clear the inside rods (See Figure 2.1).

You may use any rod or reel with a large enough line capacity. However, I would not recommend spooling your reels with under fifteen pound test. The reason for this is in-line planers put an added stress on the line while being pulled or fighting fish. A good tip that will keep you from losing your whole rig in the event of a break off, would be to use lighter line from the split ring or stop to your lure. If you do break one off, it should only break the leader instead of the fishing line itself, thus saving your in-line device.

Unlike other planer board setups where I prefer shallow or deep running body baits, both body baits and spoons fish equally well on in-line planer boards. There are several in-line planer boards on the market today. There are two that I have used and have had excellent success with. One is the "Yellow Bird Side Planer" that will carry your lure one hundred and fifty feet or more to the side of the boat when trolling. It is fairly small, only 7½ inches long and 3 inches high, and comes equipped with a release. If you hear fishermen at the dock or on the radio talking about taking fish on their "Birdies," this is what they're using. Another good planer is the Wille "Sideliner." This one features a reversible arm so it can be run on either side of the boat, an orange flag so other boats can see where your planers are, and comes equipped with its own release. It is slightly larger than the "Yellow Bird," being 9¼ inches long by 3 inches high.

Using Downriggers

When trolling in the Great Lakes no matter what time of year or depth of water you're fishing, downriggers will produce fish. When trolling in the top forty feet of water, I will usually run my lures fifteen to thirty feet behind the downrigger weights. Just like when fishing the beach in the early spring, I will run my outside downriggers shallower than the ones on the stern of the boat. Fish closer to the surface will often move to one side of the boat or the other as it approaches them, while deeper fish will have less of a tendency to spook away from the boat. As in most downrigger fishing, the majority of your fish will be taken on spoons. So as not to repeat information, in the next chapter I will talk about the proper downrigger weights, releases, rods, reels, and line to use. I will also cover downrigger patterns and how to hook the fish that hit on them.

Diving Devices

Another method of catching fish that are too deep for planer boards, flat lines, or in-line planers besides downriggers are diving devices that attach directly to your fishing line. Divers have both advantages and disadvantages to that of downriggers. The advantages are the ability to set them to run off to the side of the boat and being able to run more deep lines without adding downriggers to your boat. They also create added action to your bait which can be very helpful during calm (flat) weather. Their disadvantages are that divers are hard to fish in rough seas because they might put too much action on your lure and larger divers pull too hard on the rod in the set position for light tackle. There are smaller divers available for lighter outfits but they won't go as deep. My favorite diver is the Luhr Jensen size 1 "Dipsy Diver." It is completely adjustable. This diver can be run on either side of the boat with a dial to adjust how far to the side it runs. It can be tripped both from the boat or by a fish when it strikes, and it comes in a variety of colors. The depth your "Dipsy Diver" is running is regulated by the length of line you have out. This holds true for most diving devices. Most manufacturers furnish charts with their divers to show the amount of line needed to reach a desired depth. Refer to these charts to regulate the depth of the diver that you will be fishing.

I fish my divers in two ways -- either in a rod holder off the side of the boat more towards the bow from the outside downrigger, or I run them off my outriggers. Outriggers are long fiberglass or metal poles that hold fishing lines out to the side of the boat with a release mechanism. For running divers you need strong sturdy rod holders because of the severe pull when they're in the set position. And, it is possible to run two or more divers on each side of the boat by using ones that are adjustable as to how far they run to the side. Adjust the outside diver to pull out farther than the inside ones do. A good example would be when fishing two Luhr Jensen "Dipsy Divers" on one side of the boat, run the outside one on the #3 setting and the inside one on #1 1/2. Just like in planer board or in-line planer fishing, put the outside diver in the rod holder closest to the bow of the boat and the inside one in the rod holder towards the stern. During the summer months I usually use my outriggers to run one diver on each side of the boat. During this time, most of my lines are fished deep where the fish are congregated in the cool water. However, some species like steelhead or coho salmon might be laying above the cool water column and are taken on these rigs.

With limit catches of lake trout being quite common in some ports, a couple of big steelhead or a coho or two can greatly enhance your catch. When using diving devices like a size 1 "Dipsy Diver," it is very important to use rubber snubbers between the diver and the bait. A snubber is a shock absorber made of colored surgical tubing that softens the impact of the strike. They will keep you from breaking off fish when they hit or when the diver is out of the water and the fish are thrashing on the surface near the boat.

To rig a diver tie your diver's release mechanism to the fishing line, then use a six to eight foot leader from your snubber to the lure (See Figure 2.2). Never have the leader longer than the rod you're using because it will make fish hard to reach when you're going to net, gaff, or release them at the boat. My favorite outfit for running divers off the side of the boat would be a nine to ten foot medium heavy action rod and a powerful reel with a good handle. My favorite reel to use would be a Diawa SG 47 LC which is larger than the line counter reel I use for planer board fishing. Because heavier line is used, reels with a large line capacity are required. Line counter reels work great on divers because you know how much line you have out to

Figure 2.2
Dipsy Diver Rigging

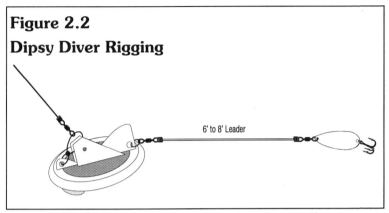

6' to 8' Leader

control the depth they're running. For larger divers your line should be at least twenty pound test to the diver, and slightly lighter between the snubber and the lure. This will keep you from losing the whole rig if you break a fish off. When fishing them off the outriggers, I like the same reels and lines. However, since the rod itself isn't helping to hold the diver away from the boat, a shorter lighter rod can be used.

Hot Baits

Here's a list of hot baits that I would use for different methods of fishing described in this chapter. For planer boards and flat lines use body baits exclusively. Top producers are Storm 1/2 & 1/4 ounce "Hot-N-Tots" and 3/8 ounce "Wigglewarts." The best colors are metallic silver with a blue herringbone, metallic silver-florescent green herringbone, metallic silver-florescent red back, metallic gold-black back, metallic gold-florescent orange back, all orange, and all chartreuse. 3/8 ounce "Rattlin' Fatraps" in chrome with a red belly, orange crawdad, or fire tiger. And 1/2 ounce "Tadpollys" in metallic silver-florescent red herringbone (Bloody Mary), and metallic silver-blue back.

For in-line planer boards, both body bait and spoons will take fish. All of the body baits just mentioned will also work on the in-line boards. My favorite spoons are "Northern King" size NK28 and C5 in hammered silver-gold prism tape with chartreuse scallops, hammered silver-orange laser tape with orange vinyl scallops, hammered silver-blue prism tape with pearl scallops, florescent green-orange laser tape with orange vinyl scallops, chartreuse-orange laser tape with orange vinyl scallops. "Pro-King" spoons in silver-purple prism and black vinyl tape, silver-green prism and chartreuse vinyl tape, silver-cracked ice orange and silver prism tape, silver-cracked ice orange and gold prism tape. The Renosky Lure Company "Pirate Spoon" in size #55 and #44 in colors hammered silver-orange laser with orange vinyl scallops, hammered silver-green prism with chartreuse scallops, chartreuse-orange laser with orange vinyl scallops, white-pink prism with red prism scallops, and one of their airbrush painted finishes -- metallic blue with black bars. Magna-Dyne "Northport Nailers" in both the magnum and standard sizes in colors white with red prism tape, black with red prism tape, white with orange prism tape and white scallops, chartreuse with orange prism tape and chartreuse scallops, and silver with light blue prism tape and dark blue prism scallops. All of the spoons just mentioned also work great on your down-riggers.

On diving devices, both spoons and plugs will take fish. However, I feel spoons usually work better. Some fishermen will attach a three way swivel on their snubber and fish both a spoon and deep diving body bait behind it. Use a six foot leader with a deep diving body bait and a four foot leader with a spoon. This will help prevent tangles. This technique might work for you when you want to get more lures in the water and are limited to a number of rods. My cousin, Denny Allen, who has the boat the "Never Miss" out of Saugatuck, Michigan found out the only problem with this technique is when two big steelhead hit on the same rod breaking the rod holder in two and swimming away with everything.

Choosing Lures

With all the different color and size lures available, here are a couple tips to help you choose which ones to use under different conditions. On sunny bright days, use silver lures or lures with combinations of silver and color that will reflect light. On overcast days or during low light conditions, use gold or dark colored baits that will absorb the light present. To know what size of lure to use, try to duplicate the size of bait fish existing in the area you are fishing. Another important factor on choosing lures is to find ones that compliment each other on trolling speed. Some lures work well when trolled slow, others when pulled faster. Do not try to pull both types of lures at the same time.

In some harbors during certain times of the year, your catch might consist of all one species of fish. Examples of this would be fishing in early April at New Buffalo,

Michigan which is located in the southern end of Lake Michigan. There your catch would be made up of nearly all coho salmon. When a fish is hooked, you know it will result in another spring coho in the box. Another example would be T-bar or thermal barrier fishing fifteen to twenty-five miles offshore at Ludington, Michigan located in the northern part of Lake Michigan. This would take place during the late summer where your catch would be all steelhead.

These are both great places and times of the year to fish, but for me and many of my customers, having great fishing and not knowing what's going to hit next adds a special element of excitement to the trip. Water temperatures in the top forty feet are at or near what is preferred for most species of salmon and trout. So, during spring offshore fishing you might hook a triple and have three different species on at once. This is very common in May and June on Lakes Michigan, Huron, and Ontario. Another reason late spring fishing can be a special time for me is because after fishing near the beach in the early spring, it feels great to head out to the open clear blue water.

CHAPTER *3*

SUMMER TROLLING TECHNIQUES

Because there are so many methods and locations to catch salmon and trout during the summer, I will break them down into locations. Then, for each one I'll explain how to fish them using different techniques and the best lures for different situations.

Fish will be found on thermoclines, around mid-water schools of bait, along the bottom, and on thermal barriers caused by a change in surface water temperature or where different currents meet. When fishing thermoclines and mid-water schools of bait, downriggers will produce many of your fish. There are many different makes and models of downriggers on the market. All of them, except for mini downriggers, will work for this kind of fishing. Mini downriggers are basically designed for shallow water,

Fisherman with a big summer king salmon caught aboard the "Can't Miss" while fishing deep with downriggers.

rivers, and inland lakes. They are not built to handle the heavy downrigger weights needed for this type of fishing.

For deep fishing, I prefer cannonball style weights. Downrigger weights that have fins or are flat in shape have a tendency to be pushed sideways by the current causing lines to get tangled more frequently. A twelve pound cannonball style weight works well to depths over one hundred feet, and will not drag back too far behind the boat. Lighter weights will drag back too far, making it hard to estimate how deep your weight is actually running.

My favorite downrigger release is the "Walker Adjustable Line Release." It can be adjusted so you will have ample pressure between the rod and the release. However, with the adjustment set light, even a smaller fish will be able to pull it free. When fishing deep with downriggers, you will have a lot of line out between the rod and the lure. Because of this, I feel that it is important to have the release set tight enough so that when a fish hits, it will drive the hook into its mouth before releasing the downrigger. Then get to the rod quickly, reeling up any slack line before the hook can be worked free from the fish's mouth. In most cases, when using proper release tension, setting a hook when the fish hits a downrigger is not necessary.

A good choice of fishing rods would be seven to eight foot light action fiberglass or graphite rods equipped with level wind reels. Spinning reels can also be used but will have a tendency to twist up your line when the drag is being pulled from the reel as the weight is lowered. The reels should have a large enough line capacity to stop big fish and be loaded with twelve to twenty pound test monofilament line.

Downrigger Weight Patterns

While working thermoclines and fish suspended around mid-water schools of bait, I use two different downrigger weight patterns depending on the depth zone that contains the proper water temperature to hold fish. A thermocline is where warm and cold water meet at a certain depth below the surface. Sometimes this change of water temperature will be quite drastic. When this occurs, the zone or band of water that contains the preferred temperature for salmon and trout will be very narrow. Under this condition when using five downriggers, I would only have them spread out over an area of fifteen feet in depth. When using four -- only ten feet. On my boat, the "Can't Miss," I use five downriggers and call this an "M" pattern (See Figure 3.1).

When fishing this pattern I have my outside downriggers (outdowns) and middle downrigger five feet below the two located on the boat's stern corners. On the outdowns and center rigger, I run "Add-A-Lines" that are attached to the fishing lines three to five feet above the weight. The procedure to rig an "Add-A-Line" is to set the

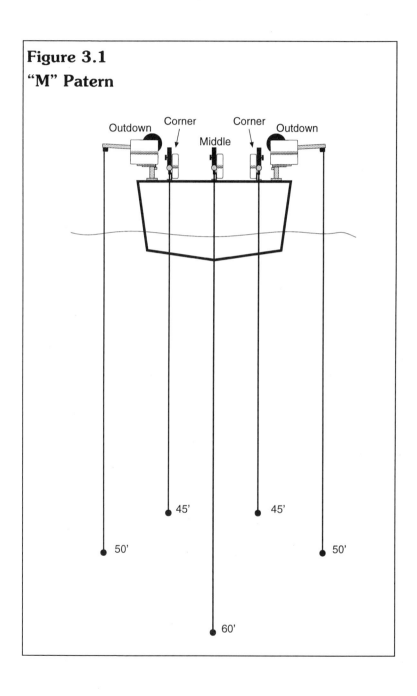

Figure 3.1
"M" Patern

Outdown Corner Corner Outdown
Middle

45' 45'

50' 50'

60'

main line off your downrigger release, then lower the weight into the water. Then three to five feet above your downrigger release, attach a small rubber band to the fishing line leading to your rod by forming a half hitch with the rubber band around the line. The half hitch will hold the rubber band in place so it will not slide up or down the fishing line. An "Add-A-Line" leader should be approximately six feet long with a snap swivel and lure on one end and a snap on the other. Insert the snap through the rubber band and attach it to the fishing line. Then drop your lure overboard and lower your downrigger to the desired depth and your "Add-A-Line" rig is set. When a fish hits an "Add-A-Line" it will break the rubber band sliding the snap down the line to the release. Then when it releases the downrigger, the snap will slide down the line and be stopped by your lure (See Figure 3.2).

With your main bait set back as far as twenty feet behind the release, it's very important to get to the rod and reel very quickly to tighten up the line on the fish. There's an easy way to tell if the fish has hit the main line or "Add-A-Line" while watching your rods. When a fish hits an "Add-A-Line" instead of the main line, he will be hitting

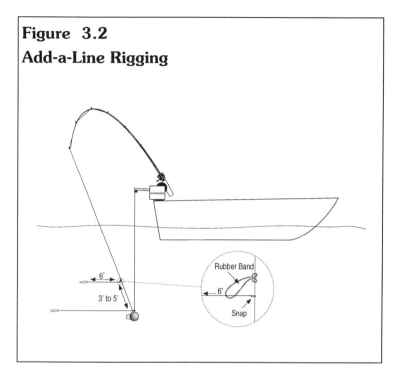

Figure 3.2
Add-a-Line Rigging

against the rod itself and the strike will appear to be much more severe than when it hits against the release.

A good downrigger pattern for fishing a wide band of preferred water temperature with five downriggers would be a deep "V" (Figure 3.3).

An example of this would be having your outside downriggers set at sixty feet, your corners at seventy, and your middle rigger at eighty. With "Add-A-Lines" five feet above the weight on all of your downriggers, you would

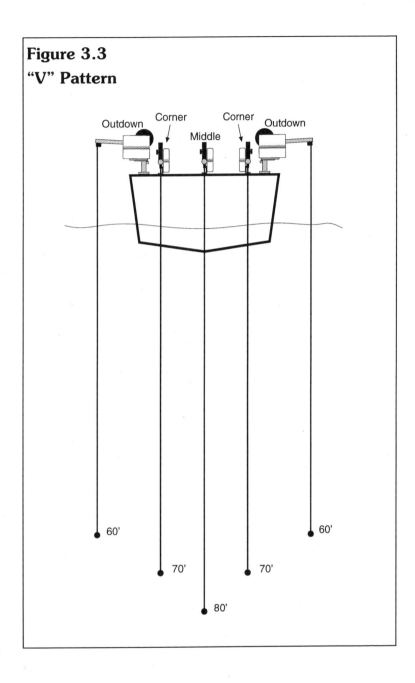

Figure 3.3
"V" Pattern

have two lures at fifty-five feet, two lures at sixty feet, two lures at sixty-five feet, two lures at seventy feet, one lure at seventy-five and one at eighty. With a spread like this, you will be able to present many different types and colors of lures over a wide band of water at the same time.

Like in all trolling with multiple lures, run ones that compliment each other on the speed they're being pulled. My best lures for mid-water fishing with downriggers on the main line of the downriggers are Magna-Dyne Magnum "Northport Nailers" and "Wobbler Spoons" in colors white-orange vinyl tape with white scallops, chartreuse-orange vinyl tape with chartreuse scallops, white-red prism, black-red prism, and silver-light blue prism tape with dark blue scallops. "Northern King" NK 28's in colors hammered silver-gold prism tape with chartreuse scallops, hammered silver-blue prism with pearl scallops, florescent green-orange laser tape with orange vinyl scallops, chartreuse-orange laser tape with orange vinyl scallops. Lake Products #3 "Charger" in colors florescent green-silver v (Green Machine), white-florescent red dots, white-florescent green v, and chartreuse-florescent orange dots. The "Little Tuffer" in colors white-pink prism tape with pink vinyl dots,

Optimum Temperature Zones for Freshwater Game Fish

Brown Trout	60-68 degrees
Crappie	65-75 degrees
Coho Salmon	50-58 degrees
King Salmon	48-56 degrees
Lake Trout	44-52 degrees
Largemouth Bass	75-80 degrees
Muskellunge	65-75 degrees
Northern Pike	65-75 degrees
Perch	58-64 degrees
Smallmouth Bass	65-70 degrees
Steelhead (Rainbow Trout)	58-62 degrees
Striped Bass	62-68 degrees
Walleye	62-70 degrees

florescent green-white vinyl tape with florescent green dots, and florescent green-red prism tape with florescent red dots. On "Add-A-Lines" I prefer lighter, smaller spoons. My favorites are "Lucky Lures" in hammered silver-florescent green, hammered silver-chartreuse, and hammered silver-florescent red. #22 "Sutton Spoons" in hammered silver-gold (brass) back. Magna-Dyne standard size "Northport Nailers" in the same color patterns as just mentioned with the magnum size.

Using Drop Sinkers

A method of fishing that produces over three hundred fish per year on the "Can't Miss" when they're midwater is using drop sinkers on flat lines. For drop weights I use one pound lead balls attached to the fishing line with a Big Jon "Jettison Sinker Release." When a fish strikes, the sinker drops and the release slides back to the lure. This release allows you to run the weight as far ahead of the lure as desired, and still be able to reach the fish while landing them at the boat. I would suggest using eight to ten foot medium to medium heavy action rods and level wind reels filled with twenty pound test monofilament. Long rods will help you keep your drop sinker out of the way when fished in rod holders off the side of the boat and shorter rods work well for flat lines off the stern. Unlike downriggers when a fish hits a drop sinker, it's best to set the hook because it's usually out a long way behind the boat and doesn't have as heavy a weight for the fish to strike against. Any good spoon will work using this highly productive method of mid-water fishing. However, a hot set up for me is a size O "Luhr Jensen Dodger" with a "Jon's Fly Squid" on a twenty inch leader behind the dodger. This dodger/squid combination is my favorite when fishing king salmon, and will also take them when pulled behind downriggers. My favorite color combinations are a silver dodger with a florescent green-green insert squid, a chartreuse dodger with a florescent green-clear insert squid, and a white fishscale dodger with a blue glow squid.

Lead line outfits with weighted color coded nylon also work well for a mid-water presentation. Nylon lead core line is color coded with the color changing every thirty feet. It's available in twelve to forty-five pound test. For most applications, eighteen pound test is usually sufficient.

Because you can count the number of different times the color changes, you will know how much line you have out. This eliminates the need for line counter reels or other methods described earlier to determine the amount of line out. Lead core has a fairly large diameter, so large capacity level wind reels should be used. Never use spinning reels. They will twist and damage the line. A good choice of rods would be an eight foot medium action one with ceramic guides. The smooth ceramic guides will help prevent wear of the braided nylon coating that protects the lead center. More detailed information about different types of rigging for lead line will be explained during the chapter on walleye fishing. They are fished like drop sinkers but because the line itself is weighted, either no weight or a lighter keel weight sinker is required. This highly visible color coded line may spook fish, so it's best to use an approximately 50' long leader. Any good spoon or body bait will work for lead line fishing.

When using diving devices, employ the same tackle and techniques as described in Chapter 2, but with more line out allowing them to fish deeper. Refer to the chart provided with your diver to estimate the depth it's running.

If there's steelhead or coho salmon around, run your best lures for them shallower than your other ones used on your divers. Because when fishing deep most of your catch will consist of lake trout and king salmon, a couple of coho or steelhead will significantly add to your catch.

Fishing the Bottom

Bottom fishing is a technique that proves to be particularly productive for lake trout and occasionally salmon during the summer months. Since you are bouncing your weights and lures on the bottom, areas with erratic changes in depth or rocky bottoms are extremely hard to fish. An ideal area to troll in would have a sand or mud bottom, and be fairly consistent in depth when trolling parallel to the shoreline. When fishing with downriggers, I like to have at least half of my weights occasionally bumping the bottom. Fishing a boat equipped with two downriggers I would have them both occasionally bumping, and with four downriggers two occasionally bumping the bottom. My boat the "Can't Miss," like many Great Lakes trollers, is set up with five downriggers. I run my center and outside downriggers (outdowns) bumping the bottom, and my stern corner downriggers ten to fifteen feet off the bottom. Using "Add-A-Lines" on my deepest rods, I can run eight lures in the bottom ten foot of water putting all of them in a productive zone for catching fish that are tight to the bottom. A good method of trolling using this technique of downrigger fishing on the bottom, is to angle slightly towards the shoreline until your downriggers begin to bump bottom then turn out until they stop, repeating this trolling pattern. Most of your strikes will occur either after your weights first hit the bottom or stop bumping when angling away from the shore. My father, Captain Bob Peel, referred to bouncing the bottom as "kicking sand in their eyes" which results in stirring up the bottom making game fish think bait is present or that other game fish are actively feeding. Any good downrigger lure will work. However, silver or combinations of silver and color are the best. Because fish can see florescent green at extreme depths, lures with a combination of silver and florescent green have produced most of my fish for many years while bumping the bottom.

Other rigs that are very productive for this type of fishing are attracter lure combinations. Using a dodger with a spoon or peanut twenty-one inches behind it or cow-bells which are in-line spinner blades pulling a lure twenty-one to twenty-four inches behind them. Cowbells and dodgers should be silver in color so they'll flash and attract fish that will strike the lures trailing them.

Mike Glaspie, owner, and Captain Kim Slayer from the sportfisherman "Reel Hooker Too III," fish the entire west coast of Michigan. In their travels to many different ports in Lake Michigan, they have picked up and shared with me some valuable tips they have learned from local fishermen in the various ports they have visited. One is their use of wire line rods for fishing lake trout on the bottom. Using a one pound weight on twenty pound test wire, they let out enough wire until the weight (sinker) is consistently bouncing on the bottom. The weight can be attached to the wire with a sinker release that will drop (release) it when a fish strikes or by using a three way swivel and tying the weight to the three way with a light piece of monofilament line. Then the weight will only be lost when it gets snagged on the bottom, breaking it off only and not losing your entire rig. From the sinker release or three way swivel, tie a six to eight foot leader that you will use to attach your lure to the wire line. A good choice of rods would be a seven to nine foot medium action one with a roller guide tip equipped and a large capacity level wind reel. Mike and Kim feel that since wire line rods are fished on flat lines, longer rods will enable you to maneuver fish under the wire line stretched out far behind the boat much easier. Their best lures for wire line fishing are light spoons with a combination of silver and color. Mike and Kim are both excellent fresh water fishermen and have to date landed many trophy game fish including two over-thirty-pound chinook salmon.

Thermal Barriers

Thermal barriers (T-Bars) develop throughout the Great Lakes and are fished quite often during the summer. Because there is so much information on fishing techniques for T-Bar fishing, a separate chapter is needed. Summer trolling with its many styles of fishing and warm wonderful days, make it a great time to be on the water whether you're working mid-water schools of bait, bouncing the bottom for lake trout, or offshore T-Bar fishing your chances of taking fish with their many available locations is terrific.

A summertime mixed bag of salmon and trout.

CHAPTER *4*

T-BAR FISHING
THE STEELHEAD EXPLOSION

Thermal barriers, commonly called T-Bars, are found throughout the Great Lakes and other large bodies of fresh water in the spring, summer, and fall. During the spring, they will contain all species of salmon and trout because the surrounding water is cooler containing a variety of fish. In the summer and fall when the surface water is warmer, they will hold nearly all steelhead which prefer warmer water than other species of salmon and trout.

T-Bars are formed when warmer in-shore waters meet colder offshore waters. Then a vertical wall of water called a thermal bar is produced. There are many ways to locate them depending upon the equipment you have available on your boat. If your boat is equipped with a surface temperature gauge, you will see from a few to several degrees drop in temperature while heading offshore. This will

One of many nice steelhead caught in a day that a productive T-Bar was located.

occur in a short period of time or distance traveled. For boats with or without a surface temperature gauge, there are several other ways to locate T-Bars. Look for a change in water color, current swirls, a drop in the air temperature, or floating debris on the surface of the lake. Two other ways that I find much less trustworthy are looking for slicks (smooth water surrounded by ripples) and watching for feeding birds. Slicks can be caused by many different occurrences taking place in the water and birds might be feeding wherever bait fish are near the surface.

Locating Thermal Barriers

After being off the water, even if only for one day, try to remember what prevailing winds were present. This will give you some idea where to relocate the T-Bar you had been fishing which are often moved by winds. To take locating T-Bars even one step further, some fishermen employ the technology we've learned during the space age. There is a service available that shoots infrared photos from a NOAA weather satellite. This information is fed into a computer that transposes it onto charts showing different surface water temperatures all over the world. Then it is sent to subscribing fishermen at their boats or docks via fax machine. Subscribers to this service will get enlarged charts of the areas they're going to fish. The only drawbacks of this service are the cost involved and the inability of the satellite to take pictures under cloudy conditions.

T-Bar Techniques

After a T-Bar is found, there are many different ways to fish it including planer board systems, in-line planer boards, diving devices, downriggers, and flat lines. The best trolling pattern is a zigzag one, making forty-five degree angles back and forth across the thermal barrier. When targeting steelhead, a trolling speed from two and one half to three and one half miles per hour will produce more strikes and allow you to cover a larger area of water. When trolling faster, set your drag tension lighter than for normal trolling speeds.

Steelhead hit very hard and jump almost immediately, so a lighter drag will keep the fish from tearing off or breaking the line on the initial strike. After the fish is under control, the drag can be firmed up so you will be able to gain line and control the fish near the boat. Steelhead jump very high and cartwheel in the air similar to tarpon in saltwater! A good tip to help eliminate break-offs at this time that is used by tarpon fishermen is to bow to the fish. This is done by facing the fish and bending at the waist which lowers your rod tip as the fish jumps, thus eliminating undue pressure on the fish while airborne. Another tip that will help you land more steelhead and all other fish is proper boat speed after the strike. When a fish hits and is burning line off the drag or pulling very hard, slow the boat immediately. If it is swimming with the boat, maintain your speed to keep some pressure on the fish. When it's charging the boat, you might have to increase your speed accordingly. As you can see, steelhead fishing is not only exciting, it can also be very challenging.

Now, let's go over the different techniques for the presentation of lures while fishing thermal bars. Planer board systems, which were discussed in detail in the chapters on spring fishing, are very effective ways to present body baits to fish near the surface. In the spring, they will catch a variety of salmon and trout, but in the summer and fall nearly all steelhead. Good diving body baits will work for a variety of fish, but my best ones when targeting steelhead alone are Storm "Hot-N-Tots" and "Wiggle Warts" in colors metallic silver-florescent green herringbone, metallic sliver-blue herringbone, and florescent orange. Another top producer is the Heddon "Tadpolly" in the colors silver-blue back, and silver-florescent red herringbone (Bloody Mary). The sizes of these lures should vary depending on the bait fish or food present. When fish are feeding on insects and young of the year bait fish, small lures will outproduce larger ones.

The use of in-line planer boards was also explained in the spring fishing chapters. I feel, as many other fishermen do, that they are much better when targeting steelhead than a standard planer board set up. This is because of their effectiveness while using spoons which track much truer at faster trolling speeds required for steelhead. My hot spoons for steelhead pulled behind these are "Northern King" NK 28's & C 5's in colors hammered silver-gold prism tape with chartreuse scallops and hammered silver-orange laser with orange vinyl scallops. The Renosky "Pirate Spoon" in size 55 or 44 in colors hammered silver-light blue prism tape with dark blue prism scallops and hammered silver-light green prism tape with chartreuse scallops.

Diving devices that will take the lure down without the aid of a downrigger, generally outproduce downriggers when fishing steelhead near the surface. The one I recommend, because of its ability to be adjusted so it will run out to either side of the boat, is the Luhr Jensen "Dipsy-Diver." Run them in sturdy rod holders located on the side of your boat with nine to ten foot medium action rods and level wind reels filled with twenty pound test monofilament line. With only fifteen to twenty-five feet of line out, in clear water you will be able to see your "Dipsy-Diver" and lure running under the surface out to the side of the boat. Because of the short distance this device is run from the boat when fish strike, they'll jump so close you'd swear you'd be able to reach out and touch them! The same spoons that are run on in-line planers fish great on "Dipsy Divers." With the addition of Magna-Dyne standard and magnum size "Northport Nailers" in colors white-orange vinyl tape with white scallops, chartreuse-orange vinyl tape with chartreuse scallops, and black-red prism tape (Black Budweiser).

Downriggers can also be fished shallow for steelhead by using the "V" weight pattern described and illustrated in the summer trolling techniques chapter. Good lures for them would be the ones just mentioned for in-line planers and divers. When present, salmon and lake trout can be caught by fishing downriggers deep along thermal bars. A good downrigger weight pattern would be the "M" pattern fished in conjunction with "Add-A-Lines" as described in Summer trolling techniques.

Steelhead are found throughout the Great Lakes, and from California to Alaska along the west coast of the

United States. They are caught offshore in open water and in and near rivers where they congregate to spawn. According to several different sources, as of 1989 Lake Michigan has become the best steelhead fishing in the world. This is due in part to improved stocking methods by the Michigan Department of Natural Resources, and Lake Michigan anglers pioneering and perfecting T-Bar fishing.

Catch rates on steelhead by Lake Michigan charter captains have gone up from less than seven percent of their total catch of all combined species in 1988, to nearly thirty percent in 1992. Hooking a scrappy steelhead in the deep blue offshore water can be the thrill of a lifetime. When these big beautiful fish hit, they are airborne before you can get to the rod. You don't have to hook them, they'll hook you!

CHAPTER **5**

FISHING FALL SPAWNING RUNS

Chinook salmon, coho salmon, and steelhead trout are anadromous fish. This means that they spawn in fresh water, but migrate to the sea for feeding and maturation. This is as true for the Great Lakes as it is in the ocean, except the lakes provide the area for them to feed and mature, and the tributary rivers and streams for them to spawn.

Understanding Stocking Operations

Chinook (king salmon) are planted from the hatchery as six month old spring fingerlings. They offer anglers a chance to catch them for the next three and one half years, then spawn and die. Their spawning runs will usually begin in August by staging (congregating in front of rivers) in the open lake or bays off the streams and rivers where they were either planted or naturally reproduced. Then, in late

Author with big fall spawning king salmon.

August or September when the natural urge to reproduce overwhelms them, they will enter the rivers or streams to spawn.

According to a recent study conducted by the department of fisheries and wildlife from Michigan State University, statistics gathered indicate that over thirty percent of the chinook salmon presently being caught in Lake Michigan are naturally reproduced fish. At one time biologists and fisheries management personnel thought that all salmon would have to be raised in hatcheries and stocked (planted) into the Great Lakes. Findings from this study indicate that chinook salmon will always reside in the Great Lakes even without a stocking program for this species. This study has only been conducted in Lake Michigan, so the amount of native fish in the other Great Lakes is not yet known.

Coho salmon are planted as eighteen month old smolts. By the next spring, they will grow to three pounds. During the next six months, they will feed heavily and triple their weight by fall. In Lake Ontario where bait fish are plentiful, twelve to fifteen pound adults are not uncommon with an occasional fish growing even larger. Coho show up off streams and river mouths where they were planted in September and run (migrate up) them in late September and October. Many anglers like to fish for coho because they are much easier to catch than wary finicky chinooks. Unlike chinook salmon, there is no evidence that coho naturally reproduce in the Great Lakes. Coho, like all Pacific salmon, die after spawning.

Steelhead, which are the last anadromous species to come in during the fall spawn, have grown in numbers due to the improved stocking methods in the Great Lakes. Different state agencies used to stock steelhead as six month old spring fingerlings with an approximate two percent return on these plants. Through research, these agencies found that by holding fish longer in the hatcheries, like coho salmon, their survival rate was greatly improved. The result of this has been an astonishingly improved return of over thirty percent in some stocking locations.

Like king salmon, many steelhead are also derived from natural reproduction. Steelhead generally show up near their spawning tributaries in late October and November, migrating upstream through the winter. The timing is such that when they begin to spawn, the salmon are done. Skamania (summer run) steelhead is a subspecies that has been introduced into the Great Lakes. Unlike other strains of steelhead, they spawn during the summer months. Unlike salmon, all steelhead don't die after spawning but some do succumb due to stress from their ordeal in the rivers and streams.

Spawning Run Patterns

The timing of spawning runs can be affected by weather conditions. An abnormally cold summer can cause salmon and steelhead to spawn somewhat earlier than they would under a normal weather pattern. A hot late summer and fall with a sudden cold snap, can make for a short fast run of salmon. If abnormally warm weather persists into the fall even if the water temperatures are far above their preferred temperature zones, salmon and steelhead will eventually spawn anyway as their biological clocks tick down. Many salmon have been caught by anglers in seventy degree water as they school up in front of rivers and streams for their spawning migration.

When trolling for fall salmon and steelhead at river mouths, there are two locations to fish. The first, which would be good early in the morning or late in the afternoon, would be close to the mouth of the river or stream itself. Where rivers with pier heads empty into a lake, the current forms a hole at the end of the pier head with a sandbar outside of that. This hole, and the outside slope of the sandbar, will hold a good number of fish waiting to migrate upstream. Most boats will be trolling parallel to the shoreline going back and forth in front of the harbor trying to hit these spots as many times as possible. On the occasion that boat traffic is light, trolling into the river current can produce strikes from fish that are otherwise hard to entice. Now before you get to the outside sandbar as you approach the hole, slow your trolling speed and let the current coming out of the river give your bait action. This will hold your bait over a salmon and steelhead much longer aggravating them enough and many times will result in a strike. Because most boats will be unaware of this trolling method to entice reluctant fish to hit, they will continue their normal trolling pattern. This will make it nearly impossible to troll in and out without being cut off by the other boats. That is why this trolling pattern is only possible during light boat traffic.

Body baits are generally best for this technique of enticing salmon and trout to hit. This is very similar to the technique called "drop back fishing" that anglers use to take salmon and steelhead while anchored in rivers below damns. At rivers and streams without pier heads, similar strategies can be used. However, shallow water depths generally limits fishing to small boats.

The second location to fish occurs as the sun gets higher in the sky or too much boat traffic is present. Some fish that are ready will head up the river and others will move out to deeper more secure water. In most harbors, the fish that move out will generally end up in thirty to fifty feet of water. They might be anywhere from near the surface to hugging the bottom, so fish with both high lines and downriggers.

Fall Fishing Equipment and Lures

Here's the equipment that I use to take fish during the fall, and the best lures to use in conjunction with it. Because boat traffic is usually quite intense during the fall run, instead of planer boards I use outriggers. Planer boards can be a problem in crowded fishing conditions because of their distance out to the side of the boat. They will get tangled in other fishermen's lines and will even get run over by other boats. Good outriggers are fifteen to twenty feet long and made of either fiberglass or aluminum, they have adjustable holders that allow them to be run nearly horizontal. It's important to have an adjustable release mechanism that allows the fishing line to run through it, so changes in the distance a lure is run behind the outrigger can be made without bringing the release to the boat. Set the release tight enough so a fish will have to pull back on the outrigger before it releases. This will help set the hook before the outrigger releases because a release can cause slack line before you can get to the rod. The distance to run your lure behind the outrigger should be determined by the intensity of fishing pressure and weather conditions that are present at that time.

Under crowded conditions, run them shorter most of the time so that they will not interfere with other fishermen. On bright flat days, run them back further even if many other boats are trolling in the area. With a combination of bright sunlight and heavy boat traffic, the fish will become even more spooky and be difficult to catch on short leads. When trolling in this situation with long leads, use more caution when approaching other boats looking and planning ahead for a clear spot in the pack to troll through. On an outrigger, I would consider a short lead one hundred feet and a long lead one hundred and fifty feet.

A good choice of rods would be your light to medium action seven to eight foot planer board rods, with line counter reels. The line should be clear or light pigmented fifteen pound test low stretch monofilament. My favorite body bait for this type of fishing by far is the Storm 1/2 ounce "Hot-N-Tot" in colors metallic silver-florescent green herringbone, metallic silver-blue herringbone, all chartreuse, and white with black dots. Another good body bait is the Heddon 1/2 ounce "Tadpolly" in colors silver, chartreuse, and florescent red with black dots.

Flat lines are also productive, and like in spring fishing, do well fished off small boats. I would use the same rods, reels, line, and lures as just described in outrigger fishing. Small boats often use spinning rods for flat line fishing which work fine if lead lengths are estimated properly. When running a combination of outriggers and flat lines, I generally run the flat lines slightly shorter to keep them from getting tangled in the outriggers while making turns. Otherwise, they should be fished the same distance behind the boat as you would outriggers under the different conditions. When a fish hits a flat line, since he's not striking against any release pressure that is present with outriggers or downriggers, it's best to set the hook immediately.

Diving devices also work well on salmon and steelhead at this time of year, with the Luhr Jensen "Dipsy

Diver" being the best. They should be fished shallow with the side adjustment set at #2 1/2 or #3 so they will run as far to the outside of the boat as possible. If two are run off one side of the boat, the inside diver should be set at #1 1/2 and the outside one on the #3 setting. Use the same rods, reels, line, and hooking techniques as described in the chapter on T-bar fishing steelhead. Some fishermen working the harbor mouth at Pentwater, Michigan when fishing adult steelhead in the late fall, have had some outstanding catches using this technique. It gives these boats good maneuverability allowing them to stay in the most productive water.

Any good salmon or steelhead spoon that you have confidence in will work pulled behind your divers, but ones with larger hooks will hold fish better. For colors, use the standard rule of bright baits for sunny days, and dark ones for low light conditions.

Downriggers work great in the fall, especially for salmon. When fishing near the harbor mouth, use a shallow water weight pattern similar to that of early spring with the outside downriggers shallower than the ones on the stern of the boat. The only difference might be running them a few feet deeper because fall salmon have a tendency to be nearer the bottom than spring fish. When you move out to deeper water during the midday, downriggers will become your most important piece of equipment. At this time of day, the use of deep or bottom fishing techniques explained in Chapter 3 will catch fish while other fishermen assume they're shut off. Use an "M" downrigger weight pattern with the outside and middle riggers below the corners. Add-A-Lines will take fish on your deep lines, like they do during the summer months. Use the same rods, reels, and line on your downriggers as you would for summer fishing. One exception to this would be when fishing in an area where mostly large chinook are being caught. Twenty pound test line, instead of fifteen pound, might be more suitable.

My best spoons for salmon and steelhead on the mainline are Lake Products #3 "Chargers" in colors florescent green-silver v and white-florescent red dots. Three eighths ounce Luhr Jensen "Rattle Snakes" in gold and silver, and blue and silver. Magna-Dyne magnum "Northport Nailers" in colors white-orange vinyl tape with white scallops, chartreuse-orange vinyl tape with chartreuse scallops, and silver-light blue prism tape with dark blue prism scallops.

On the Add-A-Lines, I like "Lucky Lures" in colors silver-chartreuse, silver-florescent green, and silver-red. I also do well on like standard size "Northport Nailers" in the color patterns just mentioned for the magnum sizes.

Another lure that works well especially for fall salmon on downriggers are #3 and #4 Luhr Jensen "J-Plugs" in colors silver (silver bullet), gold, pearl, and chartreuse. These plugs will dive and kick up sand with the weights run a few feet off the bottom. Like with other bottom bouncing techniques, this can result in strikes from finicky fish. "J-Plugs" should be run farther behind the weight than spoons, both enhancing their action and giving them enough line to reach the bottom. Most of this midday bottom fishing will take place, as mentioned earlier in this chapter, in thirty to fifty feet of water.

Fishermen without boats at river and stream mouths also have excellent opportunities to catch salmon and steelhead in the fall. Using the same information provided in Chapter 1 "Early Spring Fishing," you will be able to catch fish both by casting with spoons and still fishing with spawn. For salmon you might want to use a little heavier tackle and line than as described for brown trout in the spring. Your spring brown trout rods will be perfect for fall steelhead. Active fishing for salmon usually takes place in the morning and evening. However, since steelhead are primarily midday feeders, they can be taken at any time.

The selection of castable spoons and the techniques of fishing spawn mentioned in Chapter 1, are also very effective at this time of year. Your catch will consist of mostly salmon from September to mid October and steelhead from late October until the lake freezes over.

CHAPTER *6*

OPEN WATER PERCH FISHING

The yellow perch native to eastern North America, and which has been introduced to many inland waters in America and Canada, is well known and popular as both a food and sport fish. Yellow perch are carnivorous and inhabit lakes, ponds, streams, and rivers. They spawn in the spring. The female, at that time, lays strings of eggs among water plants, branches, and rocks. They grow to a maximum length of about fifteen inches and weight of about two pounds. A little known fact pertaining to perch is that they are Perciformes. This is the largest group of fish in the world today comprising of over six thousand species that have been classified into about 150 families.

Perciform fish occur in abundance in both salt and fresh water areas of the world ranging from shallow fresh water ponds, to a depth of over seven thousand five hundred feet in the oceans. The order includes many of the

78

world's most important salt water food and game fish such as tuna, mackerel, bonitos, marlin, swordfish, and sea bass. Their fresh water cousins include the sunfish and walleye.

The most productive waters to fish perch in the Great Lakes are the open waters and bays of Lake Michigan, Huron, and Erie. The other Great Lakes, along with much of the fresh water in North America, have good populations also. They are found in a variety of bottom structure at different times of the year including rock, mud, and sand. Their diet varies according to location. Being an opportunistic feeder, they feed on mostly a variety of minnows, crawfish, wigglers (Mayfly larvae), muddlers, insects, and worms. In the spring, large females are caught in great numbers when they are feeding heavily before they spawn.

A good example of a thriving spring perch fishery would be in South Haven, Michigan which is located in southeastern Lake Michigan. The perch fishery is so good there, they even have head boats that take out from thirty to fifty passengers at a time, similar to bottom fishing party boats in the ocean. I have seen the head boat "Captain Nickols" come in with over three thousand perch on a five hour trip. At this time of the year, they generally fish in sixty to sixty-five feet of water where there is a mixture of a sand, rock, and mud bottom. Stomach contents indicate the fish are mostly feeding on alewife, smelt, muddlers, and spot tail shiners. Since these species of bait fish aren't available to the public, most fishermen use shiner or fat head minnows for bait.

During the summer, the perch seek out shallower water with a rock bottom either closer to shore or around islands and reefs. An abundance of crawfish, small alewife, and minnows will attract and hold them in this rocky structure. The optimum water temperature for perch to feed actively is fifty-eight to sixty-four degrees. In the Great Lakes when strong offshore winds blow the warmer summer water out bringing in cool water from the bottom of the lake, perch will be found in very shallow water, bays, and around pier heads at river mouths. During this time, fishermen without boats can have excellent catches of perch at pier heads and breakwaters.

During the fall, the perch will move out off of rocky bottoms and reefs into somewhat deeper water and begin to feed heavily as winter approaches. In Lake Erie and many deep water bays, fall is the best time to fill your cooler with perch.

Perch Feeding Habits

BC (Bythotrephes or the European water flea) that has recently entered the Great Lakes, provides perch a nearly endless supply of food during the summer and fall (See Figure 6.1). This small animal (less than one half inch in length) is native to northern Europe including the British Isles, Scandinavia, and the Soviet Union. The first living specimen in the New World was found in Lake Huron in December 1984. The most likely mode of transportation was in fresh water or mud brought to the Great Lakes from Europe in the ballast water of merchant ships.

By 1985, BC had spread to Lakes Erie and Ontario. It had invaded Lake Michigan by 1986 and Lake Superior by 1987. Michigan Sea Grant researchers claim that the quick success of BC in colonizing all of the Great Lakes raises the possibility that it may soon invade smaller inland lakes in the Great Lakes basin and beyond. When BC is present, perch will feed so heavily on this tiny animal that their stomachs will be completely full. I feel this new source of food has caused perch populations to explode in some of the Great Lakes. However, whether they will have a detrimental effect on plankton populations and other fish communities will take years to discover.

Mayfly larvae, called "wigglers," are similar in character and size to that of Bythotrephes and because of their similarities, make an excellent bait when fish are feeding on BC. Wigglers that are naturally present in most waters where yellow perch are found have been a favorite

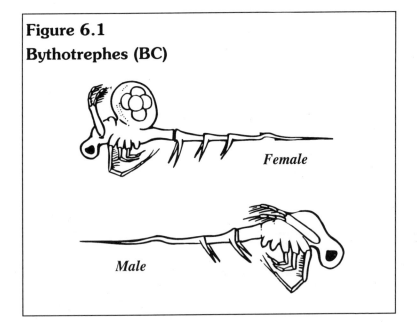

Figure 6.1
Bythotrephes (BC)

Female

Male

bait used by fishermen for many years. Now that I've covered where to find yellow perch and what they feed on, let's find out how to catch them.

How and Where to Find Them

Proper anchoring techniques and rigging play a very important part in perch fishing. Mushroom, Navy, Delta, and Grapple anchors are all good for specific types of bottoms. However, a fluke style anchor will hold in virtually all types of bottom structure when rigged properly. First, you must have the right size fluke anchor for your boat. Boats eighteen feet in length and under require at least a nine pound anchor. Eighteen to twenty-four feet -- fourteen pound, twenty-four to twenty-eight feet -- twenty pound, and twenty-eight to thirty-two feet -- twenty four pound. The anchor should be equipped with a chain that will both prevent chafing of the line while rubbing on rocks and will add weight to the front of the anchor, helping it to dig in and hold the bottom more effectively. This chain should be not less than ten feet long with a 1/4 inch diameter on vessels to twenty-four feet and 5/16 diameter on vessels to thirty-two feet. The anchor line should be at least three times as long as the depth of water you will be fishing. Boats from eighteen to twenty-four feet in length should use 3/8 inch diameter nylon line and ones over twenty-four to thirty-two feet a 1/2 inch diameter. This information is provided for you as a guide only. Please be certain to follow carefully manufacturer's specifications and weighing information when you purchase anchor lines, anchors and other hardware required for anchoring purposes.

In rough water, the length of anchor line out (scope) should be even more than three times the depth of water to hold properly. When fishing a rocky bottom where your anchor can become easily fouled or wedged in the rocks, here's a trick I learned while fishing the coral reef in the Florida Keys. Have an eye welded to the back of your anchor, then attach your chain and anchor line to it. Using a small piece of cotton clothes line, run your chain to the front of the anchor then tie the chain with the clothes line to where it is normally attached on the anchor. If your anchor becomes fouled, you can back your boat down breaking the light cotton clothesline from the front of your anchor then your anchor will be pulled backwards allowing it to come free.

To set your anchor in a sand or mud bottom, let out an amount of line three times the depth of water. Tie it on the bow cleat and apply power in reverse. If your boat moves, reset the anchor and try again. Once the anchor has been set, it will almost always hold the same amount of tension that was used to set it, even if the scope has been reduced except in rough water. On a rock bottom backing down, except to take the slack out of the anchor line, is usually not necessary because the flukes will generally catch in the rocks. Once you've learned the proper anchoring techniques, positioning your boat on good structure where there are schools of fish present and holding your position becomes easier.

Once you've found an area that contains perch, pinpointing an exact location to fish can be done in several ways. Small boats without fish finders can drift through an area until activity occurs. After hooking a couple of fish, throw a marker buoy so you can relocate their position. Motor back to the buoy and then into the current or wind past the buoy estimating the direction you will be drifting from your anchor. Lower your anchor making sure it's set, and then adjust the length of anchor line until you're even with your buoy. This should put you back on top of the fish you hooked drifting through the area.

If your boat is equipped with a fish finder, locate good bottom structure or schools of fish and then once again head into the wind or current, set your anchor and allow the proper length of anchor line out until you're back on the structure or fish.

Larger boats equipped with Loran or GPS (Global Positioning System) receivers use the same techniques as just described. However, after finding a good spot you have the advantage of being able to go back to the same location any day by storing it in the unit's memory. On the "Can't Miss," I use my Loran to fish the same rock piles and drop-offs throughout the entire perch fishing season.

When fishing a rock pile or drop-off, I always position my boat up wind or current from the downside slope. Fish will have a tendency to use the rock pile or downward slope of the drop-off as a break in the current and congregate in this area. Occasionally I will also look for schools of fish on my sounder very tight to the bottom. Many fishermen will often anchor up on large peaked schools of fish located on their sounders. These schools are most often adult alewife which are neither what they're looking for nor a good source of food for perch.

A secret I'm sure will at least double your catch on perch, is the use of a thumper or drag anchor. This is simply one half of a cement block on an anchor line lowered off the stern corner of your boat, until it just touches bottom. The movement of your boat while at anchor will cause the cement block to bounce up and down on the bottom, and be dragged back and forth stirring up the bottom. This will create an effect similar to bumping bottom with wire line or downriggers and will attract fish to your location.

Perch Fishing Equipment

Now that your boat is anchored properly over good structure or fish with the right water temperature present and your thumper is out, you're ready to start catching perch. A variety of rods and reels can be used, but I prefer light action six to seven foot graphite rods with cork handles equipped with spinning or spin cast reels. Graphite rods with cork handles will enable you to feel light strikes much better than with many other rods. For line I prefer six pound test, clear or light pigmented monofilament. Once again, as with many other Great Lakes fish, I feel florescent line spooks perch. For hooks I tie up my own snelled hooks using four to six pound test monofilament. It doesn't do much good to have six pound test on your rod and buy a commercially tied snelled hook that has a twelve or fifteen pound test leader. Light leaders will produce far more fish, especially jumbos (large adult perch), because of the way they bite. A perch will approach your bait flaring out its gills and sucking it into its mouth. Light leaders have much less resistance in the water, and will be inhaled much easier by hungry perch.

To determine what size of sinker you need, use only enough weight required to keep your sinker on the bottom. Do not tie your sinker onto the fishing line. Instead, thread the fishing line through the eye of the sinker and then clamp a split shot below it. Several years ago, an elderly gentlemen in a wooden boat looked at one of my rods rigged for perch and laughed. He said, "I bet you tie up a lot of hooks with a rig like that." He later explained to me that ninety percent of the time when you get snagged on the bottom perch fishing, it's your sinker and not your hook. After I started using a split shot below my sinker, I soon found out he was correct. Instead of losing the whole rig -- hook, line and all, I simply lost the sinker and by sliding another sinker on the line and clamping on a split shot, I was fishing again in seconds (See Figure 6.2).

Figure 6.2
Perch Rigging

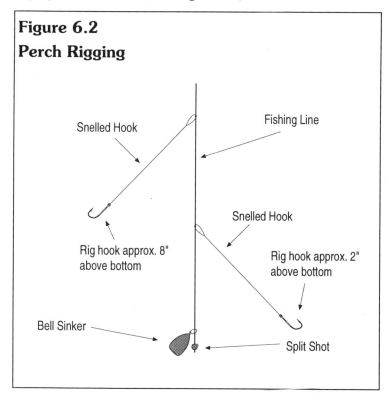

Snelled Hook

Fishing Line

Snelled Hook

Rig hook approx. 8" above bottom

Rig hook approx. 2" above bottom

Bell Sinker

Split Shot

Slip bobbers can also be used with the same rig, with a slightly lighter sinker for drifting bait away from the boat. Lower your rig down through the slip bobber until the weight just touches the bottom, attach the bobber stop at that place on your fishing line, then allow your slip bobber and rig to drift back behind the boat. Many times perch will hit this rig when it is drifting back on an open bale or spool. Both of these techniques will also work very well for crappies and many other panfish.

The live or dead bait used for perch fishing depends on the location you're fishing or the food that is naturally present. When fishing on sand and mud bottoms, I prefer shiner minnows or fat heads, if shiners are not available. Shiners are much brighter in color, making them more visible and seem to be preferred over other species of minnows when fishing perch. Wigglers will also work on this bottom especially when BC is present.

When fishing a rock bottom, minnows, crawfish, shrimp, and wigglers will all produce fish. On this bottom, it's best to have a variety of bait with you so you can use whatever is working on that particular day. When fishing a rocky bottom, I generally carry live minnows and shrimp on board. Shrimp are not native to fresh water, however, their flesh closely resembles that of a crawfish. Frozen bait shrimp can be purchased in some tackle stores, and fresh shrimp can be purchased in most supermarkets. To use them as bait, cut off the heads and peel the shells leaving just the meat of the tail. Then, cut the meat into the small pieces that you will use for bait. The heads and shells can be thrown into the water where you're fishing and works as chum to help attract fish to the boat. You will be able to catch hundreds of perch on one pound of fifty count (50 per pound) fresh shrimp at a cost of approximately five dollars. Crawfish and soft shell crawfish pinchers work well too, but they are much more expensive. In some waters, especially Lake Erie and inland lakes, worms and night crawlers will also produce fish.

Bringing Them Aboard

Hooking perch, once they bite, is quite easy in shallow water but more difficult in deeper water. When you feel or see a bite in shallow water, lower the rod slightly allowing the perch to inhale the bait with no resistance. Then, when you feel him again, set the hook by lifting the rod and reel him in. In deep water, use the same technique. However, when not having a bite for a period of time, lift your rod and if you feel extra weight, set the hook. Many times you'll have a perch on that you didn't see or feel bite. With slip bobbers, watch for the bobber to be bounced or pulled under the water. Then hesitate a moment, and set the hook.

During the early 90s, anglers aboard the "Can't Miss" averaged over two hundred and fifty perch per trip! These numbers should relate to you how effective the information contained in this chapter will be for yellow perch, crappies, and pan fish anywhere they swim.

CHAPTER *7*

WALLEYE MAGIC

Although this chapter is written primarily about large rivers, bays and open water in the Great Lakes, the fishing techniques described and the migration routes of travel for walleyes can be used for fishing them nearly anywhere in North America. Walleye, sometimes called walleye pike, are not a pike at all. In fact, they are more closely related to perch. Now found throughout the continental United States and in most of the Canadian Providences, walleye fever spreads! Explained in depth will be where to find and how to catch walleye from spring through fall, techniques that will help you catch these very popular game fish such as jigging, the proper use of slip sinkers, bottom bouncing, and the application of many new trolling devices. An entire series of books could be written on walleye fishing. Instead of covering every way to catch them, only my favorite top techniques that will put a little "magic" in your fishing will be explained.

River Fishing

Walleye will never be more vulnerable than during spring spawning runs. Male walleye are the first to concentrate in schools at traditional spawning locations. Next to migrate to the spawning sights are the large egg ripened females. This is an ideal situation for fishermen -- large concentrations of eating size males in predictable spots with many trophy size females in the same area. Because walleye will often travel as far upstream as possible for spawning, dams will stop their progress and cause them to stack up and converge at this location. Since many anglers are aware of this, fishing pressure is usually very heavy at dams.

Dams are not the only places that will hold spawning walleye. Big females will seek out breaks in the current behind rocks, logs, islands, or other obstructions in rivers and streams. Fish will also seek out and spawn in areas with a rocky shoreline where the rock protrudes out into the river on the bottom. In the spring, many walleye can be caught in rivers and streams by fishermen without boats. Fish will usually be in holes during the midday, but in the early morning and again at dusk, will be in the shallows seeking gravel bars or other hard bottom for spawning. During the night fish will also often subsist in very shallow water. Bank anglers can approach these shallow water fish much easier than their boating counterparts without spooking them. Casting a jig dressed with a minnow or a "Mister

Twister Tail" or one of the other similar type plastic tails, is the most popular method for catching fish located in shallow water.

When fishing with a boat, vertical jigging is out of the question. The movement of the boat over fish in shallow water will spook them and cause them to head for cover. Boat fishermen should remain a comfortable casting distance away from these shallow water locations and cast into the fish without spooking them with the shadow from the boat or engine noise. 1/8 to 1/4 ounce jigs with a minnow or dressed with a plastic tail for added attraction is a favorite rig for producing many pre-spawn and spawning walleye (See Figure 7.1). When using a jig/minnow combination, "Stinger" hooks with a #10 treble hook is very helpful in hooking light biting walleye. Pre-tied "Stinger" hooks with various leader lengths are available at most sporting goods stores.

During this time of year, the water is very cold and fish aren't going to slam a jig hard even when they're hungry. Because fish are cold blooded, their body metabolism and movements are much slower during periods of very cold water. Light bites are very hard to detect. And, as

Figure 7.1
Jig Combinations for Walleye

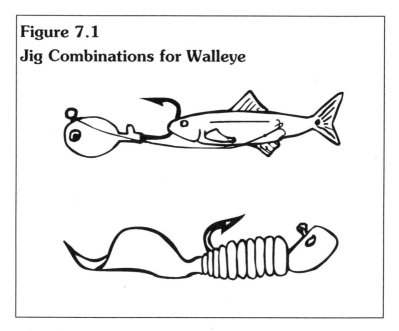

when fishing for steelhead or browntrout, anglers should use graphite rods with cork handles, which are very sensitive and telegraph the strike into your hand.

During midday fishing, walleye will have a tendency to congregate in deep holes or areas of the river with a slower current. Positioning your boat with the trolling motor or anchoring in these areas can be highly effective. If the river has a slow current flow, drifting might be feasible. Vertical jigging with a jig minnow or jig plastic tail combination is usually the most productive way to catch walleye under these circumstances. Because the extremely cold water temperature causes the fish to be lethargic, aggressive jigging motions will seldom be productive.

When fishing early in the season, you will have to force yourself to slow down your presentation. While vertical jigging it is very important to know where your jigs are in relationship to the bottom. A simple trick for knowing when the jig is on the bottom is to watch your line and wait for it to go slack on the downward jigging stroke. If the line doesn't go slack, let out more line until the jig hits bottom. If the water depth changes even a few inches, you will have to adjust the amount of line you have out accordingly.

Maintaining bottom contact is very important for early season walleye. The only effective way to entice river walleye at this time of year while jig fishing is to keep your bait within a couple inches off the bottom. Jigs and rigging for vertical jigging in deeper water are nearly the same as used while fishing the shallows. The only exception is the use of heavier jig heads from 1/4 to 3/8 ounce which will enable you to reach the bottom much more effectively. It usually takes a fairly heavy jig head to maintain bottom contact in deeper water or in waters with swifter currents.

The colors of your jigs for fishing minnows or jigs and plastic tail combinations should be bright for bright conditions and dark for dark or overcast conditions. Chartreuse is a good all around color. The next time you're watching a fishing video or your favorite fishing show on television, notice how many walleye have a chartreuse jig or crankbait in their mouth. Many experts cannot explain why, but walleye caught in nearly all waters are attracted to the color chartreuse.

Crankbaits suitable for the water depth you will be fishing will often produce spawning or pre-spawn walleye too. Casting crankbaits behind obstructions or other breaks in the current that will hold fish can be very productive. Another effective way to present a crankbait is to troll them slowly through the current on the edge of drop offs or in areas that contain rocky or hard bottoms that will hold spawning fish. The effectiveness of crankbaits on early season walleye has been proven by many steelhead fishermen who incidentally catch them while drop back fishing. Slower action crankbaits that have less side to side movement will produce more walleye in colder water. The colors of these lures under certain light conditions should be the same as just described in jig fishing.

Practice proper conservation ethics by releasing big spawning egg ripened females unless you plan to mount them. Smaller males will taste much better than larger females, and will improve fishing in the future through natural reproduction. Many smaller males will be present in the area and most are not needed to fertilize eggs for reproduction.

After the spring spawning ritual begins to subside, walleye begin leaving spawning areas in search of food and other seasonal habitat. Now it's time to move with them. Consider what circumstances will again concentrate fish in certain locations. After spawning, fish will feed heavily and the number one thing to look for is the availability of baitfish or other sources of food. Number two would be areas with good bottom structure or steep vertical drops, and number three would be places that provide good cover where walleye can hide in the shadows and ambush baitfish. One reason the fish move to other areas after spawning is heavy concentrations of spawning fish deplete the bait supply present. Once the spawning ritual is complete, fish move on in search of food and new habitat. Seasonal transitions can be puzzling. So locate prime food sources throughout the year, and you'll find and catch more fish.

Much like summer fishing salmon and trout, a wide variety of tactics can be used for walleye fishing during this season. Fish will not only hug the bottom just like during the spring, but will suspend mid-water in search of available baitfish. Prime locations will be areas that contain food and steep vertical drops on the edge of the river channel. Occasionally during periods of bright sunlight or heavy boat traffic, fish will congregate deep in the middle of the channel. This might also occur during periods of low barometric pressure or when a cold front is present.

Besides vertical jigging, here are three other ways to catch fish that are holding tight to the bottom during the summer. When anchored up or drifting in rivers with a fairly slack current, the best rig available is the "Lindy Rig." This is a walking slip sinker rig that comes with a 30 inch leader and a variety of hooks for different live bait. I would recommend size #6 or #8 hooks for leaches, #4 or #6 hooks for crawlers, and size #2 or #4 while using minnows. The size of the sinker required will vary depending on the depth of the water you are fishing, the amount of current present, or the speed of your drift. Too light a sinker will make it difficult to maintain contact with the bottom. An excellent option that is available with the "Lindy Rig" is a float system that controls the distance the bait is up off the bottom from the walking slip sinker. This option works very well when fish are suspended slightly off the bottom See Figure 7.2).

The best rod and reel to use when fishing this rig would be a six to seven foot light to medium light spinning outfit. Spinning reels work best for this method of fishing. Use an open bail with your finger holding the line. When you feel a strike, release the line with your finger. Usually let the fish take the bait until it stops and then starts again. This is the time to set the hook. When using this method of fishing, a good rule that will reward you with a higher percentage of hook ups is the larger the live bait you're using, the longer you let the fish take it before setting the hook. Walleye have a fairly small mouth for their body size and must turn large bait fish before they're able to swallow them head first.

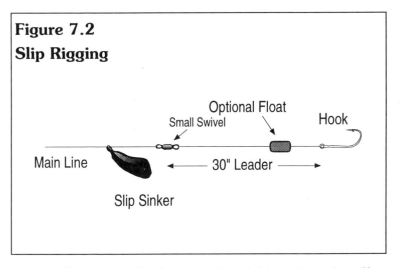

Figure 7.2
Slip Rigging

"Lindy rigging" (slip sinker fishing) loses its effectiveness in rivers where the current is too strong because the bait tends to get pushed flat to the bottom where a walleye can't see it. Even floater rigs are pushed to the bottom in stronger currents. In situations like this, or while trolling with live bait, the next two options will prove to be the most effective. While fishing in an area with a rocky bottom or many snags present, a bottom bouncing rig made of a bent wire in the shape of a "V" with one leg longer than the other. The longest leg will have the weight or sinker attached to it and the shorter one will have the leader and hook. This rig will bounce over obstructions without the sinker or hook becoming snagged. It is excellent for trolling a spinner or night crawler harness near the bottom (See Figure 7.3).

Another rig that is good for trolling, or even drifting in a strong current or wind, is the "three way" rig. This rig consists of a three way swivel with a 12 to 24 inch drop line to a bell sinker (See Figure 7.4). Like when bottom bouncing for lake trout with wire line, use a lighter leader to the sinker so only the sinker will be lost if it becomes fouled in the bottom. The leader to the hook or lure that is also attached to the three way swivel should be from 48 to 60 inches long. A variety of hooks or artificial baits can be used with this rig. Besides being able to present live bait

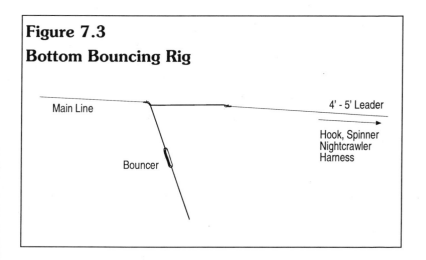

Figure 7.3
Bottom Bouncing Rig

Main Line

4' - 5' Leader

Hook, Spinner
Nightcrawler
Harness

Bouncer

Figure 7.4
Three Way Rigging

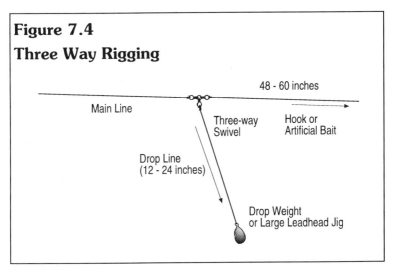

near the bottom with this rig, spinners, spoons, and minnow style crankbaits also work very well. Be careful not to use crankbaits that dive too deep or they will fish below the sinker causing them to become snagged in the bottom or obstructions.

Three way rigging has been used by walleye fishermen for many years and can be one of the most versatile options available. One thing that makes it very effective is the length of the drop line to the sinker can be adjusted to the height the fish are holding off the bottom. The only disadvantage is that it is more likely to become snagged than a wire bottom bouncing rig. With both these rigs, use a stiffer rod than for fishing "Lindy" rigs. Either spinning or bait cast reels will work fine. When a fish strikes while trolling or drifting, lower your rod tip towards the fish and when you feel him again, set the hook.

When you think about fishing with downriggers, your first tendency is to presume they're only suitable for offshore fishing salmon, trout, walleye, and saltwater species. In fact, they are an excellent way to troll in rivers where depth presentation must be very precise. During the past several years fishing on the Kalamazoo River in Saugatuck, Michigan, I have taken many trophy walleyes on downriggers. Many large rivers, as well as inland lakes, will have weeds and leaves floating on the surface. When fishing deep diving crankbaits on flat lines and estimating the depth they are running, this debris will slide down the line to the lure causing it to fish less effectively. When using downriggers, the debris will only slide down the line as far as the release and not impair the action of the lure. The ability to control the exact depth the lure or bait is fishing gives you the ability to catch fish near the bottom or ones that are suspended. Nearly any rod or reel of your choice will work for this type of fishing, from ultra light spinning to medium action trolling tackle. For downrigger weight patterns, refer to the shallow pattern described in Chapter 1 -- "Early Spring Fishing." I have my best success running lures or bait 25 to 50 feet behind the downrigger weights. Because a walleye's mouth tears easier than a salmon or trout's, it's best to set your downrigger release tension lighter than you would for other species. Too heavy or tight of release pressure can tear a walleye free from the hook before the downrigger is released.

The most common mistake I see watching anglers troll in rivers is not using the proper trolling speed in relationship to the current. Because they're watching the bank of the river and it appears to them that they are going very fast traveling downstream, they most often troll too slow in that direction. When trolling downstream you must troll faster than the current to give your lure proper action. When going into the current or upstream while watching the shoreline, it will appear that you are trolling very slow. When many anglers notice this they will speed up causing their lures to be pulled too fast into the current. Be aware that the flow of the current is providing added action to your lures while trolling upstream. So, go slow and let the current work for you. My favorite lures for this style of trolling are minnow type plugs like the Rebel "Fastrac" size #9 in colors silver black back and gold florescent orange back. "Rapala" original floating minnows sizes 11 and 13 in colors silver chartreuse back, silver blue back, gold florescent orange back, and firetiger. Occasionally spoons will be productive and my favorite one for walleye is the #3 "Loco" spoon in colors gold-gold prism, blue-silver prism, and chartreuse-silver prism. When using live bait and a night crawler harness I prefer rigs with florescent orange, florescent green, or silver spinner blades.

Trolling for walleye with downriggers on large rivers will consistently take fish from late spring through late fall. In the fall, as the cold weather approaches, the same techniques used during the summer such as jigging, bottom bouncing, or downrigger fishing will take walleye as they feed heavily to fatten up for the winter. A couple of things to keep in mind when fishing in the fall are many times fish will be feeding on larger bait fish and will concentrate in the deepest water available. For the best results use larger lures and bait fish at this time of the year to more closely assimilate the food big walleyes desire. Fishing walleye in the fall might be the least productive season of the year for numbers of fish, but can offer you the opportunity to take a large trophy fish.

Bays and Open Water Fishing

For tips and techniques on fishing large bodies of water and bays, I'm going to use the highly productive methods employed by many of the knowledgeable, successful fishermen of Lake Erie. Even though Lake Erie is a large body of water, fishing in bays like Saginaw Bay (on Lake Huron) is very similar. The only differences are the depth of water and shorter migration routes of travel for walleye. Lake Erie has an estimated population of over 30 million walleye. Because of the wide variety of forage base (food for fish), walleye can be found near the bottom or often suspend around schools of mid-water baitfish. Due to this wide variety of forage, many different techniques are used to take fish.

In the spring, fish congregate in the eastern and western basins of Lake Erie. The fish are found in these basins because the shallower water warms more quickly attracting a wide variety of baitfish and contains suitable habitat for spawning. Most of the spring fishing takes place less than five miles from shore where fish congregate on reefs or in deep waters that surround them. Like in river fishing, when the season first gets under way a jig and minnow combination is one of the most effective ways to take early season walleye in cold water. Remember once again to slow down your presentation allowing less active fish time to take your bait. To be more successful, use the same rods, reels, jigs and jigging techniques described earlier in this chapter.

If the fish are suspended, a hot new technique that will provide you with unbelievable results is planer board fishing. There are two types of planer boards used. First, the board and mast type that allows you to run multiple lines out to each side of the boat off one planer board. Second, the in-line planer boards that are attached directly to the fishing lines where one bait is run behind these smaller boards. For the proper way to run multiple lines off the board and mast set up, refer to the text and illustrations in Chapter 1 -- "Early Spring Fishing" for the most effective and trouble free use of planer boards. Because this type of fishing was pioneered in the Great Lakes for salmon and trout, fishermen visiting Lake Erie introduced this technology to the walleye fishing industry. For the proper use of in-line planer boards refer to the text and illustrations in Chapter 2 -- "Offshore Spring Fishing for Kings, Lakers and Steelhead." In-line planer boards, which are one of the hottest methods to catch offshore steelheads in Lake Michigan, are becoming very popular for catching suspended walleye in Lake Erie.

When fishing walleye with planer boards, nearly all fish will be taken on deep diving body baits. It is important to know how deep the particular diving body baits you will be using run. Select ones that will be running at the depth the fish are suspended. Quite often, walleye can be suspended below even where the deepest diving body baits will run. Because of this, Lake Erie anglers have come up with a unique way to run diving body baits deeper than they're designed to run without using heavy weights or sinkers ahead of the lure. This method is called "segmented lead core line fishing." It is used primarily behind both types of planer boards. Depending on the desired depth you need to obtain, add one, two, or three 10

yard sections of 18 pound test lead core line to your monofilament lines to increase lure depth. Splice in the section
of lead core about 50 feet ahead of your lure using two nail
knots to connect the lead core to the monofilament leader
and the monofilament line on your reel (See Figure 7.5).
This in-line sinker now takes a crankbait from 25 to 50 feet
down allowing you to catch deeper suspended fish with
planer boards. Unlike a sinker that has to be placed closer
to the lure, you can reel the lead core line through the rod
guides allowing you to use much longer leaders that will
prevent you from spooking fish in clear water.

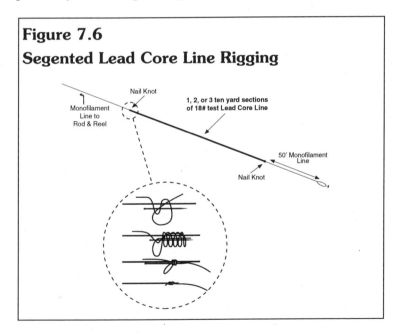

Figure 7.6
Segented Lead Core Line Rigging

For a good choice of deep diving body baits, many fishermen use Storm 3/8 ounce "WiggleWarts" and 1/2 ounce "Hot-N-Tots." For longer thinner minnow style body baits, productive ones are "Rapala Original Floating Minnows" in sizes 11 and 13, and the always popular Bomber "Long A." For using the proper color lure for the amount of light present or different water clarity conditions, use chartreuse, green or gold in low light or murky water and white lures or ones with a combination of silver and color in clear water or bright light conditions. Once again, as with jig heads or any other lure used for walleye, chartreuse without a doubt is the best all around color. When trolling with multiple lines under any light or water clarity conditions, have at least one chartreuse bait in the water at all times.

In the late spring as summer approaches and the water warms, the walleye will begin to migrate out of the eastern and western basins of Lake Erie into the deeper waters of the central basin. The geographical location to let you know where the central basin is located would be on the south shore of Lake Erie from Sandusky, Ohio east to Erie, Pennsylvania. On the northern shoreline from

Wheatley, Ontario east to Port Rowan, Ontario. When these fish move into deeper water and are positioned near the bottom, the bottom bouncing rigs and techniques described earlier in this chapter will consistently produce fish both while trolling or drifting. Also the proper use of downriggers, wire line, planing devices and segmented lead core line explained throughout this book will produce walleye all summer long in the deeper water of the central basin.

Many anglers still fish only the traditional way in Lake Erie by drifting with weight forward spinners such as "Erie Dearies," "Toms Lures," or other weight forward spinners tipped with night crawlers. During the late spring and early summer this can be an excellent way to catch many walleye with a minimum amount of equipment required. These weight forward spinners can be fished off nearly any rod or reel you have available with 8 to 10 pound test monofilament line. This technique of drift fishing and vertical jigging is quite simple. Position your boat upwind from structure or a school of fish and drift through it. Cast your weight forward spinner and crawler slightly towards the direction of the drift. Leave the bail or spool open on your reel and allow the bait to drop to a desired depth where fish are congregated. To know the depth of your lure and bait, this is a good rule to follow. A 3/8 ounce weight forward spinner on 10 pound test line drops at approximately 1 foot per second. If the fish are suspended at 15 feet, you can count down one thousand one, one thousand two, one thousand three, etc. until you get to one thousand fifteen. Engage the reel and lift your rod from nine o'clock to twelve o'clock reeling very slowly. Repeat this slow pump and retrieve process until you feel that your bait is "out of the fish" or too close to the boat. Most of the time fish will hit the weight forward spinner when it's falling back. When you feel a fish hit, reach towards the fish with your rod allowing him to take the bait then when you feel him again, set the hook. This method of drift fishing is often referred to as the "sweep" because a desired curve in the line is created that adds action to the lure and changes the direction, speed and depth of the bait as the boat drifts past it while being retrieved. Hot colors for weight forward spinners are chartreuse or green in low light or murky water conditions and white, red or silver in bright light or clear water. Weight forward spinners are available with silver, gold or painted spinner blades.

As the summer progresses, walleye will feed more selectively and will mostly be caught during the early morning and late evening. As the fishing becomes tougher, more sophisticated methods as used in salmon and trout fishing must be employed to consistently produce fish. Like in rivers, walleye will often seek out the deepest water available in the fall. They will feed on larger bait fish to fatten up for the winter. In Lake Erie, like in many other large bodies of water, this can make it extremely difficult to catch a large amount of fish on a trip. However, you do have a significant chance to take some trophy fish during the fall. Use the information in this chapter to make you a better walleye fisherman wherever you fish. It might be in one of the western rivers that are now becoming abundant with walleye, the many reservoirs throughout the midwest, the remote and wild lakes of Canada or right here in the Great Lakes. Use this information to become a highly successful and productive fisherman for these fine eating and very popular game fish.

CHAPTER **8**

HANDLING THEM AFTER THEY'RE HOOKED

Once you've hooked a big fish, your job has just begun. Many trophies are lost due to poor boat handling procedures or landing mistakes. Do you know how to maneuver your boat differently when a fish hits going downwind rather than into the wind? Are you familiar with common mistakes made while netting fish? Many fishermen land average game fish, but always seem to lose the big ones. If you're making mistakes that are costing you the exceptional ones, this chapter will help you eliminate most of your heartbreaking moments. Also covered will be tips on how to troll without tangling lines, fish cleaning, and how to package them so they'll stay fresh in the freezer.

Either when fighting fish myself or watching other anglers do battle, I've noticed that having your quarry tangled in other lines greatly distracts from the pure pleasure of landing a big salmon, trout, or walleye. Many times the fouled lines occur before the strike has even taken place by making a bad turn or trolling the wrong direction in a strong wind or current. The following poor boat handling procedures are the top five most common mistakes made while trolling that usually result in tangled lines.

1. Turning too sharp for the equipment you're using. When using multiple long lines on planer boards, flat lines, and outriggers, more gradual turns must be used. While fishing deep with downriggers, drop sinkers, or wire lines, a more gradual turn must also

be used. More fishermen foul their lines at this time than under any other presentation of trolling.

2. When turning into the wind not increasing power halfway through the turn to maintain the proper trolling speed. This will cause your progress to stop or nearly stop and run the risk of your lines becoming tangled.

3. Trolling broadside to a strong wind will result in slipping of the boat. This will make all of your lines run off to the windward side of the boat. While setting a rod on the windward side, it will usually become fouled if your course is not corrected. The same problems will occur while trolling broadside in a strong current, as they do with wind.

4. Not maintaining boat speed while trolling into wind or waves. Many times a gust of wind or big sea will stop the forward progress of your boat causing lines to become fouled.

5. Another factor that will cause lines to become tangled is an improper trolling direction in relationship to the wind or current. Try to avoid these common boat handling mistakes that will both frustrate you

and fill your garbage can with ruined, discarded line. Not to mention valuable lost-forever fishing time.

Knowing what to do with your boat and other lines when a fish is hooked usually is learned through experiences and blunders while on the water. I've watched many boats pull all their other lines immediately after a fish is hooked. This is usually not necessary unless a fish is foul hooked or extremely light tackle is being used.

Here are some reactions of fish on the line and how you should react to land them without problems occurring. If a fish hits and charges the boat, turn away from the side of the boat it is heading and increase your speed if necessary. By turning away, this will move your other lines out of the fish's way. If it's getting ahead of the boat, increase your speed to catch up. Most often after you've caught up to the fish, it will run away and behind the boat and normal landing techniques can take place. If a fish is stripping line off your reel and enough drag tension is set to put maximum pressure on the fish without breaking the line or tearing the hook from the fish's mouth, plus you've reduced your trolling speed as much as possible, you must turn on the fish. Make a gradual turn towards the direction the fish is running off to the side of the boat. Turn enough so that it is to the side and slightly ahead of the boat but not directly off the bow. Be sure your speed is not too fast so the angler won't be able to keep up with the fish creating slack line. Once you've gained enough line and the fish is under control, go past it so it is behind the boat and resume normal landing techniques off the stern.

When trolling downwind or at a fast speed and a fish begins thrashing or spinning on the surface, it's best to slow the boat immediately. I will often put the boat in reverse, stopping it momentarily. I call this "putting the brakes on." This maneuver will usually get the fish swimming again and keep the hooks from being pulled out of its mouth or breaking the line while it's thrashing on the surface.

A fish that hits and sounds diving near or under the boat can create serious problems especially when fishing with downriggers. If this happens, speed the boat up trying to keep the fish out of the downrigger cables. Once the fish is behind the boat and well clear of the cables, slow the boat and resume normal landing techniques.

One of the worst possible times and places for a fish to strike is on the inside of a turn. Every fisherman should be prepared for such instances since it will happen quite often. This occurs because inside baits will slow down enticing fish that are following them to strike. To avoid problems, get to the rod as quickly as possible, reel until the line is tight, and set the hook -- even on a downrigger. Once the fish is hooked, with the rod high walk to the stern of the boat which enables you to clear all the other lines.

Fish that hit the rods on the outside of a turn, like coho salmon and steelhead often do, usually don't present a problem. Many fish hit baits when they slow down in speed, but steelhead and coho seem to get aggressive and attack them when the bait speeds up. Fish that hit in tight turns and multiple hook ups can cause pandemonium on the back deck. My dad used to refer to these occurrences as "Chinese fire drills".

Netting fish without unnecessary complications can be made easy by following three simple rules.

1. Net them head first. Fish can't back up! If you try to net a fish "tail first" while trolling, he will quite often swim or jump out of the net.

2. Don't drag the netting material in the water. This will often result in the netting becoming tangled in the hooks causing them to be pulled from the fish's mouth. Unnecessarily reaching for a fish with the net will often have the same results. To net a fish properly, place your hand closest to the hoop and hold the back of the net with your index finger. Then when scooping the fish, release the bag of the netting while sliding your hand up the handle and scooping the fish in one fluid motion.

3. Take the fish on the side of the boat it wants to go to. There is usually a good reason that while it's next to the boat a fish wants to go in a particular direction. They could be influenced by current, wind, or hooked in the opposite side corner of their mouth. If you try to force them to the side of the boat that they do not want to go, they will often dart under the boat and break your line, especially if the fish is spooked.

Using a gaff hook can be an effective way of landing large game fish when done properly. Like with a dip net, take the fish to the side of the boat it prefers to go.

Then with the hook pointed down, reach over its back and stick the fish well below the dorsal fin, pulling it into the boat with one fluid motion. Gaffing fish has the advantage of being able to land ones that are too large for your net and not having to untangle fishhooks from the netting. However, the disadvantage is the mess on board caused by bleeding fish.

Practicing Proper Conservation Ethics

Sport-minded fishermen in most parts of the world practice some form of catch and release. There is no need whatsoever to kill more game fish than you wish to consume. To provide a strong sports fishery for ourselves and our children, we should practice ethical conservation of this valuable resource. Releasing fish unharmed is easier off of small boats than large ones because of your ability to reach the water. If you can reach the water from your boat, a good way to release them is by removing the hooks with a pair of needle nose pliers without touching the fish. This will be accomplished much easier when the fish is tired or played out.

Nearly all fish are protected by a slime coating over their scales or skin. The removal of that slime by wiping or rubbing it off can result in the growth of fungus which will eventually kill the fish. A good way to minimize this when netting a fish is by wetting the entire dip net bag and a spot on the deck were the fish will be placed. After the hook is removed, gently pick up the fish and slide it head first into the water. If a fish is hooked extremely deep and bleeding, its chances for survival are greatly reduced. These might be the ones you want to keep for your table or freezer. Remember, the practice of releasing unharmed fish to propagate or be caught again will produce long term benefits for generations yet to come.

In the Great Lakes, coho salmon have no natural reproduction and grow to full size eighteen months after being planted. Because of these factors, there's no need for catch and release on adult coho salmon. The species that should be protected the most in these waters are lake trout that grow very slowly and don't spawn until they are at least seven years of age. In Lake Michigan, biologists estimate a twenty pound lake trout to be approximately twenty years old with an average growth rate of one pound per year.

Preparing Your Catch

Most fishermen know how to fillet or steak fish. So instead of providing you detailed information on how to clean them, I'll explain why it should be done in a particular way. When large fish are filleted, they should be skinned and have the belly fat removed. There are two reasons for this. First, it will greatly enhance the flavor of the fish. The second reason is according to John Hesse of the Michigan Department of Public Health, "Preparing fish for the table in this manner will reduce any contaminates that are present by over fifty percent."

Steaking fish is an excellent way to prepare them for the broiler or the outdoor grill, especially for salmon. Steaks should be no more than three quarters of an inch thick with the skin left on and belly fat trimmed. During broiling and grilling, fat will be cooked away and drip either into the broiler pan or coals on the grill. Steaks prepared properly are both pleasing to the eye and delicious.

When cleaning small fish like perch and pan fish, skinning and trimming is unnecessary because of their low fat content. Most fishermen feel that pan fish are much better eating scaled with the skin left on.

Here's a way to package large fish fillets and steaks for the freezer that is used in many fish markets that sell them as fresh. Wrap fillets or steaks individually in clear Saran Wrap or any other cling wrap. Then, lay them flat on a cookie sheet and place them in the freezer until frozen solid. Next, place several individually wrapped pieces into a one gallon zip lock bag and return to the freezer. You might have to cut large fillets into pieces before wrapping so they'll fit in the zip lock bags. One advantage of individually wrapped fillets and steaks is your ability to use only the amount required for the number of people you're serving. An excellent way to freeze perch and other pan fish is to place the desired amount required for a meal in a one gallon zip lock freezer bag and then fill the bag with enough water to completely cover the fillets. Vent all air remaining in the bag and place it in the freezer. This method of freezing will keep fish very fresh and help eliminate freezer burn.

A Note on Contaminates in Fish

Regarding fish contaminates, I would like to enlighten you on information I've obtained from two different sources. According to a statement by seven Michigan State University scientists convened by the MSU Center for Environmental Toxicology, this statement was in response to a draft brochure circulated by the National Wildlife Federation on June 28, 1989. "The carcinogenic risk assessment approach used by the National Wildlife Federation is not appropriate because it includes a number of assumptions that do not appear to hold for the contaminates of concern in Great Lakes fish. Among the inappropriate assumptions are:

1. The susceptibility of humans to PCB-induced cancer is identical to that demonstrated in rats and mice.

2. The activity of PCB as a carcinogen is equal to that of the most active carcinogens known to cause cancer in humans."

Limited studies of persons inadvertently exposed to relatively high amounts of PCBs and related compounds, such as PPBs and Dioxins, suggest humans are less sensitive than laboratory animals. Studies of PCBs in laboratory animals indicate that they probably do not cause cancer by damaging genetic material as do many of the most potent human carcinogens. These data, in combination with other research results, suggest that the risk to humans of PCBs are greatly exaggerated by the method employed by the National Wildlife Federation. The same conclusion holds for the pesticides mentioned in the NWF document.

The public should understand that while it is not possible with current knowledge to accurately predict the risk of cancer from eating Great Lakes fish, it seems clear to the knowledgeable toxicologists at Michigan State University that the risk is small and likely to be negligible when fish consumption is part of a varied diet.

My second source of information is written by John Husar and printed in the Chicago Tribune on Sunday, July 2, 1989. The appropriate title to this article was "Lake Michigan Cancer Scare is Pretty Fishy." I will only quote Mr. Husar in a couple paragraphs of his very informative article. "For very strong yet oblique political reasons, the nation's largest conservation organization has embarked on a campaign to ignite the fear of cancer in you and me, whenever we go fishing in the lakes.

"Now, I suppose you're wondering why the 5.8 million strong NWF would want to impose these fears on us. Well, for that we have to consider the power-broking world of Washington, for this group is one of several environmental organizations jousting for supremacy."

Information provided by these two sources should help you identify some of the hocus pocus and politics involved in fish eating advisories. In my opinion, subservient organizations like the NWF have put undue pressure on state agencies resulting in much more stringent fish eating advisories than are actually necessary. Very little press has been given to the fact that contaminant levels in Great Lakes fish have been drastically reduced by over 90% since the 1970s.

CHAPTER **9**

RIGGING YOUR BOAT FOR MAXIMUM EFFICIENCY AND MINIMUM MONEY

Knowing what type of equipment you will need for a particular species or location you will be fishing can be difficult. Rigging a small boat that will be used for near shore fishing doesn't require equipment as expensive as one heading offshore looking for T-Bar, steelhead, or deep water walleye. With the help of Bill Bale, who is an expert on electronics and balanced rigging techniques, we will guide you on what to purchase for different fishing applications. This information will both save you money spent on unnecessary items and turn your boat into the "ultimate fishing machine."

Rods, Reels, Line, Lures, and Bait

This information is explained in depth in the chapters on different species or seasons of fishing. Refer to the Index for the location of this information in the book.

Fish Finders

Fish finders, in some ways, are improperly named. They should also be called structural locators. These machines are used for different methods of fishing including still fishing, drifting, and trolling. Besides locating schools of bait and game fish, they simulate bottom structure and pinpoint thermoclines. In this section we are going to cover three different types of fish finders beginning with flashers. Flashers are basically a narrow eyed fish finder used for locating changes in the bottom content such as a ledge or drop off, and used as a quick reference for depth.

LCDs (Liquid Crystal Displays) come in a variety of different frequencies or kilohertz (KHz). Different frequencies allow you to fish various depths of water and get maximum definition out of your machine. LCDs with higher numbered frequencies are designed for shallower water use. Frequencies in these units vary from 450 KHz to 50 KHz. They are ideal for small boats because the display screen is easy to read in all light conditions, plus they have back lighting for nighttime use.

LCDs have two different mounting options. Either a permanently installed unit that runs off the twelve volt system on your boat, or portable units that are ideal for fishermen to use when renting a boat or fishing on a friend's boat that does not have a fish finder. Portables are a valuable tool for anglers who travel to different locations to fish with rental boats and still want the highly important ability to find fish, depth, and bottom structure. These portable units can also be very effective for ice fishing by simply making good *liquid* contact between the transducer and the surface of the ice.

Here's a reference guide as to which frequency LCD you should use for your type of fishing. The 50 KHz frequency is basically designed for deep water use. It will provide you with good definition and clarity in depths of over 100 feet with a maximum depth of over 2,000 feet. The next frequency down from 50 KHz is 120 KHz which is a midrange frequency with a wide angle of transmission for shallow water definition and a maximum viewing of the bottom. The 200 KHz unit is designed for shallower water use of basically less than 100 feet. Transducer cone angles tend to be a little narrower down to 20 degrees giving you better definition of the bottom. The 450 KHz models are designed for extreme shallow water use in depths less than 50 feet deep. This shallow water unit gives you maximum definition of the bottom and is used mostly in rivers and inland lakes. Use this information to obtain the LCD best suited for the waters you will most often be fishing. If you fish in a variety of water depths, the midrange frequency (120 KHz) would be the best for you.

Video fish finders, employing Cathode Ray Tube technology (CRTs) are used primarily in open or deep water. However, they have a disadvantage in open boats because the display screen is extremely hard to read in sunlight, similar to trying to watch TV while the sun is shining through the window, fading out the picture. Regardless of the problems occurred in viewing the display screen by open boats, video fish finders are still by far the most popular for open water fishing in the Great Lakes. The reasons for this are their ability to work well in deep water and their outstanding mid-water definition. Mid-water definition is very important for Great Lakes anglers who mostly target suspended fish. The ability to define the difference between plankton, bait fish, and game fish is of the utmost importance. A good video fish finder which is properly installed to eliminate sunlight glare is a necessary tool for open water fishermen. They are well worth the extra expense you will pay over the cost of an LCD or flasher when targeting salmon and trout.

Navigation Aides

Navigation aides are not only necessary in open water situations, but can be very beneficial in inland waters and river systems. We are going to touch on a few of the basic aides including compasses, Loran-C, plotters, Global Positioning Systems (GPS), and radar. The compass is a very beneficial instrument that should be on all boats, regardless of their size or the bodies of water that they will be operating on. After installing a new compass or making changes in equipment on your boat near the compass, check it to make sure it's reading true north. You need to have extreme confidence in your compass when visibility becomes limited or when running in unfamiliar waters where you can become confused by junctions in the channel or areas containing shoals or islands.

Card type compasses which many of us are familiar with are the most widely used and have models that are very affordable. The disadvantage of this type of compass is unnatural magnetic forces aboard your boat may cause some deviations in your compass causing it to read incorrectly. To help avoid this situation be careful not to place metal objects too close to your compass. Some of the less expensive models of card style compasses will often suffer from lag, spin, or over swing while the boat is turning. This will cause them to be somewhat less accurate, but still adequate for smaller boats.

There is a much more expensive electronic compass available called "Fluxgate" that electronically reads the earth's magnetic field many hundreds of times a second and transmits this data to a microprocessor in the display unit. Your heading is then displayed on a large LCD readout with no lag, spin, or over swing. Now that more manufacturers are producing these units, the price has gone down significantly. However, they are still quite expensive and not a necessity on most boats. Even for offshore fishermen, a high quality card style compass is sufficient.

Loran-C is a navigation device that operates off radio towers that transmit a signal which is picked up by the receiver that separates the earth into latitude and longitude lines. It positions your boat accordingly in milliseconds that are updated every second giving you an accurate location of your present position. Loran-Cs are used basically for big (open) water navigation. However, they are also beneficial for navigation in inland lakes and rivers. For offshore fishing or on big lakes where you have no landmarks to bring you back to a desired location, using latitude and longitude numbers it gives you a compass heading and distance back to your hot fishing spot. All makes and models have memory capabilities and most are able to store up to one hundred of your favorite fishing locations.

Plotters, which are used in conjunction with the Loran-C, are also a very helpful navigational tool that draws out on an LCD or CRT screen a progression of dotted lines showing where your boat has traveled. This gives you an advantage over a Loran-C by not only giving you a compass heading and distance back to your hot fishing spot, it also presents an exact line of travel to reach this destination.

Global Positioning Systems (GPS) receivers are similar to Loran-Cs but instead of receiving their signals from radio towers, get their information from satellites orbiting the earth. This information is translated into latitude and longitude by the receiver giving you your exact present position anywhere in the world. The units are usually used on extremely large bodies of water or where Loran-C transmission signals are weak or non-existent. One advantage they do have, even in areas with good Loran-C reception, is their ability not to be affected by adverse weather. Sometimes during thunderstorms, you will temporarily lose your Loran-C transmission from a tower. GPS units are very expensive and until prices come down, most boats will continue using Loran-C or combination Loran-C/Plotter receivers.

Radar is an instrument designed to be your eyes during low visibility conditions. They are most important when operating in fog and navigation aids or the shoreline are not visible. Nighttime use gives you added confidence when running in case boats are at anchor, adrift, or running without navigation lights clearly visible. To use your radar safely, make sure it is tuned properly. When running, watch the water near the bow of your boat for logs or debris that is too low to the horizon to be picked up by your machine. Radar works by sending out a signal which is bounced off an object and returned to the machine then displayed on the screen. Radar units are available with a minimum of a 10 mile range to a maximum of a 72 mile range. The smaller the range, the less expensive the radar unit is. They are also available in a black and amber screen or a color screen with the later being much more expensive. The color screens give you a little better definition as far as the density of the object you are marking, making it easier to distinguish small boats from large boats and the intensity of bad weather such as present during thunderstorms. Because of their expense, radars are used primarily on larger boats. However, some smaller units with black or amber screens are now becoming very affordable.

Temperature and Trolling Speed

First we're going to touch on water temperature starting with surface temperature units that can be bought in a variety of different options. Many fish finders come with surface temperature built into them or you can buy an independently mounted temperature gauge that works off your 12 volt system. The most inexpensive surface temperature unit available uses a 9 volt battery that is displayed on an LCD readout with the temperature probe being mounted on the stern (back) of the boat. The 9 volt unit is portable and would be good for fishermen using different or rental boats. Fish Hawk makes a hand held temperature gauge which will read surface temperature, but also gives you the option of finding the desired down temperature. It comes in a 120 foot model and a 200 foot model with a gear driven counter that indicates the depth of the probe. The 120 foot model can be purchased with a light meter that tells you the amount of light available at your desired depth. Except for surface temperature, these hand held units are designed to be used when the boat is stopped before you begin trolling.

When down temperature is important, Walker Downriggers makes the Duo Temp-Sense system. This is both Bill's and my favorite one for Great Lakes fishing. It has a digital LCD display with the capability of hooking up two Walker Downriggers to it. These are wired to give you the water temperature at the weight (ball). The signal is sent through the downrigger cable itself to the LCD display. This unit can also help you to adjust your trolling speed. If the temperature rises, you might be going too fast. When the temperature drops, you might be going too slow causing the probe to fall into deeper water as the angle of the cable is reduced. This unit does not require the large probe mounted above the weight or the stern mounted transducer as all other downrigger temperature units do.

As with temperature gauges, there are several different types of speed indicators as well. Surface speed is the most common and is found as an option in many fish finders or you can buy an independent unit which vary in expense according to quality and features offered. Most of these units operate off the paddle wheel which transmits a signal to an LCD or video display on your boat. Downrigger speed plus temperature is also available in a Fish Hawk model 840 which operates off the paddle wheel principal mounted in a little torpedo which mounts to your downrigger cable just above the weight (ball). This sends a signal to a transducer mounted on the stern of your boat and reads out on an LCD display aboard your boat. This unit reads both trolling speed at the weight (lure speed) and down temperature. For all sizes of boats, the ability to determine your trolling speed is one of the most important keys to successful fishing. When a strike occurs, note the speed for that trolling direction so it can be duplicated again after the fish has been landed. No boat that trolls should be without some type of trolling speed indicator.

Radios

Radios come in a variety of models ranging from hand held to permanent mounts. There are two different types of radios -- VHFs (Marine Band), and CBs (Citizen's Band). The VHF is a FM frequency and the CB is a AM frequency. The FM frequency is found to be much clearer and gives you a greater distance in transmission. The hand held VHF radios, as mentioned in Chapter 1, vary in power from 1 to

5 watts. A good rule of thumb is your transmission capabilities are approximately 1 mile per watt which makes them very good for small boats for safety purposes or as an excellent backup radio.

Permanent mount radios vary in price drastically. Inexpensive models have transmitting capabilities up to a maximum output of 25 watts. However, during transmission your wattage may drop to as low as 12 to 15 watts in these less expensive radios. More expensive radios will hold a true 25 watts during transmission. Antennas for these radios come in a variety of quality and sizes. Most of them are from 3 to 8 foot in length or you may add extensions to make them up to 20 feet. The higher you have your antenna mounted, the better your radio's receiving and transmitting capabilities.

Citizen's Band radios (CBs) were very common during the late seventies and early eighties because of their affordable price. Since the late eighties, CBs are not as affective because the Coast Guard no longer monitors this band. Very few boats still have them on board so you're taking the chance of reaching someone in a car, truck or a home based station if trouble arises.

Combination Units that Save Money

Available at a considerable savings are LCD or
video (CRT) fish finders with a combination of a Loran
Plotter or GPS-Plotter. They also have surface temperature
and trolling speed in all the combination units. With the
exclusion of models containing GPS (Global Positioning
Systems), they are very affordable with the least expensive
being ones with LCD displays. These units not only save
you money, they save on space allowing you to have most
of your electronics on one display screen. This can be very
useful to smaller boats because it will save on space where
room for mounting equipment is limited. The only problem
with combination units "is you're putting all of your eggs in
one basket." If they have to be sent in for repair, you will
have practically no electronics left on board your boat.

Proper Installation of Electronics

Installation of fish finders hooked to 12 volt systems
should have a fused power supply which will prevent the
unit from being damaged by a surge in power. Placement
of the transducer is very important. On transom (stern)

mounts, it is imperative to keep the transducer flush with the bottom of the boat. If there are corners or edges protruding below the bottom of your boat, it will cause turbulence and air bubbles giving you an inaccurate reading on depth. For instance, if you were in 60 feet of water, you might experience erratic readings showing the water depth to be only 1 or 2 feet. Then as the boat slows down and the turbulence disappears, the true reading of 60 feet will be displayed on your screen.

When installing navigation aides like your compass, it's very important not to place it too close to your radio which has a speaker with a magnet. This can cause your compass to spin or give false readings. When installing a Loran-C, the power supply should run directly to a battery, isolated if possible. It is very important when installing a Loran that you have a good heavy ground cable run from the unit to the ground plate on your boat or the motor block. GPS units do not require heavy grounds similar to those used on Lorans. Radars should have the power supply run directly to the battery because of the high amperage they draw. A direct ground should also be used like described for a Loran-C. The amount of power required to operate some radars is also a factor besides their high cost that limits their use to larger boats.

When installing a permanently mounted radio that requires an external antenna, your antenna should be a minimum of 3 feet from any other antenna. A fused power source must be used so in the event of a power surge your radio will not be damaged. If you are receiving interference on your radio from your fish finder, it can be eliminated by isolating the power source to your radio. For example, if both your radio and your fish finder draw their power from the fuse block on your boat, disconnect one from the fuse block and attach it directly to the battery. It's very important to use in-line fuses on any power sources hooked directly to your battery. For more information on installing electronics refer to the installation instructions provided with your equipment.

Downriggers

On small boats, C-clamp style mounted downriggers can be removed easily when they are not required. They are also a necessary way to mount them when using rental boats. If you clamp riggers on the side of your boat, never mount them farther forward than 3 or 4 feet from the stern. This could cause the cable to become tangled in the propeller and possibly damage it and the motor while making a sharp turn. Most often clamp-on mounts are only adequate when using one or two downriggers.

Another inexpensive option is to mount two to four downriggers along with a desired number of rod holders on a pine 2 x 8. This piece of wood should be as long as the stern of the boat is wide and not protrude out from the sides of the boat. When using four downriggers, the outside ones (outowns) should have at least 4 foot arms and swivel bases that can be turned in while coming dockside. The 2 x 8 with the equipment mounted on it should be clamped or temporarily attached in some other manner on the stern of the boat. When you want to use the boat for family pleasure or fishing not requiring this equipment, simply remove it. It can be reattached again when needed. Here's another mounting option that deserves mentioning for boats with recessed gunwale or transom mount rod holders. Many downrigger manufacturers make gimbal mounts that attach to the rigger allowing you to slide the mount down into the rod holder tube and be ready to use them in seconds. For large or small boats, this is the ultimate mounting technique for people who only want downriggers on their boats when needed.

If your rails or stern is high enough to make working with your downriggers comfortable, base plates that are screwed or bolted to the rails are another excellent mounting procedure. Mounting knobs can be unscrewed leaving only the base plate on the rail or stern. These plates are designed to be low profile so they're rather obscure and do not get in your way.

Downrigger boards are the best mounting methods for boats that have rails too low for comfortable operation. Bending over to reach your downriggers all day long will soon take its toll on your back. These boards don't have to distract from the beauty of the boat like an old pine 2 x 8 would. They can be made out of mahogany or other fine hardwoods and finished to bring out the grain making them an eye appealing addition to your boat. Fiberglass and aluminum ones can also be purchased. Base plates can be mounted on them for temporary removal when the downriggers are not needed or during storage of the boat.

On medium to large boats that have downrigger boards or rails high enough for easy operation, mount five downriggers. The two outside ones should have long arms of at least 4 feet and the two corners and center downriggers only need 2 foot arms. One exception to this is with out-drive boats a 4 foot arm must be used on the center downrigger so the cable will clear the out-drive unit. Arranging your downriggers in this manner will give you the best possible spread of your lines presenting lures to more fish and helping to avoid tangles.

Here are a couple helpful tips on installation of downriggers. When mounting downriggers on fiberglass or aluminum boats, use stainless bolts and backing plates for extra strength. Many fishermen not using this mounting procedure have hooked bottom with their downrigger weights and lost downriggers, rods, reels, and all into the water. For the proper wiring installation of electric downriggers, it's best to run a heavy #8 wire from the hot post of the starter to the stern of the boat. Attach it to a fuse block with enough fuses for the downriggers you will be running. From that fuse block, run a #8 ground wire back to the block of the same engine. This gives you an excellent lo-

When properly installed, quality downriggers like the Speed-trol model pictured will give you years of trouble free use.

cation to hook up your downriggers so you won't clutter your bilge with wires. Because the long lead from the hot post of the starter to the fuse block is made with heavy wire, you will only need short leads of lighter wire (#12 of #14) from the fuse block to the downriggers providing you with the best possible power supply. Most downriggers have breakers built into them, but in case of a malfunction you will have the added safety of a fuse between the rigger and the power supply.

Outriggers

On small boats a good choice of very affordable outriggers are Perko three position deck or side mount holders with 15 foot fiberglass poles. This is a popular choice for many small to midsize boats. On larger boats, you might want more expensive completely adjustable holders with 18 to 25 foot poles that can be set farther off the water in high seas and nearly horizontal during flat weather. If you don't want to pay nearly $1,000 for these top of the line holders and poles, you have another option on larger boats. Perko also makes a three position holder that will accept 18 foot fiberglass or aluminum poles that work very well on larger boats. Unless you use outriggers very often, the latter might be your best choice saving you money to be used on more needed equipment for your boat.

Outriggers should be mounted slightly behind midships where the releases can be reached easily from the fishing area (cockpit) of the back deck. Use good adjustable outrigger releases to control important release tension. Cheaper close pin style releases have no adjustment and will cost you many fish. Good releases are well worth the extra money.

Planer Boards

Planer board set ups can be the same no matter what size boat you have. Nothing will consistently catch fish near the surface like a good set of boards. They get your lines out far to the side of the boat and change lure or bait speed while turning or fishing in a sea. A planer board mast mounted on the bow of your boat with either electric or manual reels is the ideal way to run a good set of boards. The height of the mast creates a slope in the tow line from the boat to the board helping the release slide out to the board. Manual reels work well if you have easy access to the position of the mast. On boats where it is hard to get to the bow, electric (12 volt) reels are a must.

Another method of running boards without a mast and still obtaining the desired tow line height is by purchasing manual reels that clamp to your outrigger poles. With the outriggers in the up position, your tow line is threaded through an eye 6 to 10 feet up the outriggers. It is important to position the reel itself on the outrigger so it is easy to reach. Nearly every manufacturer produces these clamp on reels in manual models.

The planer boards themselves are probably the most important piece of equipment for this style of fishing. There are many makes and models on the market. The best ones are double boards (two boards hooked together) for each side of the boat. These are offset with the outside board set slightly ahead of the inside one. This allows them both to catch water creating more resistance so they will pull farther to the side of the boat. Another good feature to look for is the ability of the arm separating the double boards to collapse for easy storage. Some boards either have compartments that can be flooded with water for proper buoyancy or added ballast towards the rear of the board so it runs correctly even in waves. Other boards might be designed or pre-weighted to run properly without ballast chambers. Shop around. Prices on planer boards are becoming very competitive. Most of them, with the features just mentioned, work very well.

For planer board line releases I use and recommend the Wille "Deep Dive Tow Line Release" and the Laurvick "Visa-Grip Release" or other comparable brands that you feel comfortable with. You will also need two or three rod

Offset double planer board and inline planer board

154

holders on each side of the boat strictly for your planer boards. They should be positioned so your rods can be set in a fan with the rod tips slightly apart from each other. These rod holders are a very important part of your total fishing system. Tite Lok has a triple rod holder mounting option that is perfectly designed for planer board fishing. It is fully adjustable and very easy to install. Another good multiple rod holder that has models that hold from two to four rods is made by Big Jon. These are more expensive than Tite Lok rod holders, but have a rugged design that will withstand years of punishment.

Use the information provided in this chapter to help you select the electronics or fishing equipment that best suits your needs. Don't waste money on equipment not needed for your style of fishing. Maximize the efficiency of your boat and invest your money wisely.

CHAPTER **10**

RECIPES FROM ROXANNE'S KITCHEN

My wife, Roxanne, has compiled our family and friend's favorite fish recipes. Most are fast and easy to prepare. Fish, when properly prepared, are a low fat delicious and healthy source of high protein. The recipes she has listed have a lot of variety both with different species of fish and cooking methods. We're sure you will enjoy these great recipes as much as we have.

Perch Cocktail (appetizer)

    1 pound perch fillets

    2 tablespoons salt

    1 cup ketchup

    1 1/2 teaspoons horseradish

Bring 2 quarts water to a rapid boil, add salt. Drop 1/2 pound of the perch into boiling water. Boil for 3 to 4 minutes, remove from pot and place on paper towels. Repeat this process with the remaining 1/2 pound of fish. Make sure water is at a full boil when dropping fish into pot. Chill perch for 1 hour or till firm, in refrigerator. Mix ketchup and horseradish together for cocktail sauce, serve with fish. Tastes like shrimp!

Salmon Dip (appetizer)

> 8 ounces skinned salmon fillet
>
> 1 cup Miracle Whip
>
> 1/2 cup dairy sour cream
>
> 1 teaspoon lemon juice
>
> 1 tablespoon dry sherry (optional)
>
> salt and pepper to taste

Bake salmon uncovered for 20 minutes at 350 degrees until it flakes easily with fork. Chill fish for 1 hour or till firm. Flake fish with fork and combine all ingredients and blend well. Chill and serve with crackers. Makes about 2 cups. Great for parties! A variation of this recipe would be to substitute smoked salmon for baked salmon. If this is done, omit cooking directions.

Herb & Garlic Fish

2 pounds skinned trout or salmon fillets (scrod, snapper, or grouper for salt water fish)

1 cup Miracle Whip

1/2 teaspoon ground celery seed

1 teaspoon dried marjoram leaves

1 teaspoon dried thyme leaves

1 teaspoon garlic powder

Mix dressing and seasonings. Place fish on greased grill over medium coals or rack of broiler pan 2 to 4 inches from heat. Brush with 1/2 of the dressing mixture. Grill or broil 5 to 8 minutes. Turn, brush with the remaining dressing mixture. Continue grilling or broiling 5 to 8 minutes or until fish flakes easily with fork. Serves 4 to 6.

Roxanne's Baked Fish with Cheese Sauce

3 pounds skinned salmon, trout, or walleye fillets (snapper, grouper, flounder, or cod for salt water fish)

1 teaspoon lemon pepper

1 cup crushed Ritz or Hi-Ho crackers

1 tablespoon margarine

1 tablespoon all-purpose flour

dash of salt

dash of pepper

3/4 cup milk

4 slices of processed American cheese

Place fillets in a baking dish, sprinkle with lemon pepper and bake covered at 350 degrees for 20 to 25 minutes. Fish should flake easily with fork if done. Make sauce while fish is baking.

Cheese Sauce:

In a small saucepan melt margarine. Stir in flour, salt, and pepper. Add milk all at once. Cook and stir over medium heat until thickened. Add 4 slices of cheese and continue to cook and stir until completely melted.

When fish is done baking, pour cheese sauce over fillets and cover with crushed cracker crumbs. Place under broiler until crackers are browned. Serves 6 to 8. This dish is appealing to the eye, with a rich wonderful flavor.

Simply Delicious Broiled Trout

2 to 3 pounds skinned trout or walleye fillets (flounder, snapper, or speckled trout for salt water fish)

3/4 cup margarine

lemon pepper

1 lemon cut into wedges

Preheat oven on broil. Place fish on a foil covered cookie sheet. Sprinkle liberally with lemon pepper. Pour 1/4 cup melted margarine on top of fish. Broil for 8 to 12 minutes, or until fish browns and flakes easily with fork. Pour the remaining melted margarine over fish after broiling. Garnish with lemon wedges. Serves 4 to 6. MMM GOOD!

Capt. Ron's Charcoal Broiled Fish

4 pounds salmon or trout fillets (skin left on) (grouper or snapper for salt water fish)

Basting Sauce--

1/4 pound melted butter

1/4 cup lemon juice

2 tablespoons Worcestershire sauce

1 tablespoon Soy sauce

1 tablespoon brown sugar

1/4 cup Teriyaki sauce (optional)

1) Lay fillets on hot grill (skin side down). After 2 or 3 minutes turn fillets over, peel off and discard skin.

2) Baste often to keep the fish from drying.

3) When you suspect the fillets are 1/2 done, cut the fillet in half and check (meat will flake easily). If half done, turn the fillet and cook and baste the same length of time on the other side.

Optional:

Fillets may be marinated before cooking by placing them skin side down in a saucepan and sprinkled with Teriyaki sauce liberally. Let stand for 1 hour. Use the Teriyaki sauce in with the other ingredients for the basting sauce. This is Capt. Ron Westrate and family's favorite fish recipe for Great Lakes salmon and trout.

Grilled Salmon Steaks

6- 3/4 inch thick salmon steaks (king mackerel or blacktip shark for salt water fish)

1/2 cup butter or margarine

1 dash garlic powder

1 fresh lemon, cut in half

salt and pepper

Salt and pepper steaks on both sides. Melt butter in a small saucepan, squeeze the juice from one of the lemon halves into the butter and add one dash of garlic powder. Grill steaks directly over coals on an oiled grill. Baste with butter & lemon sauce, cooking each side till brown or fish flakes easily with fork. Serves 4 to 6. This is a favorite recipe of many natives of Key West, Florida for grilling black tip shark.

Jean Peel's Deep Fried Perch

2 pounds perch fillets (walleye, trout, snapper, and grouper can be used when skinned fillets are cut into small pieces)

4 cups vegetable oil

5 ounces commercial flour fry mix (Drakes, Golden Dip, etc.)

Rinse fish with cold water, then pat dry with a paper towel. Shake fillets or pieces in a bag with the flour mix until they are completely covered. Heat oil in a heavy deep sided frying pan or fish fryer, use high heat. Add fish and fry for approximately 3 minutes, or until golden brown. (do not overcook) Serves 6. This simple recipe was my mother's favorite for Lake Michigan perch that I enjoyed as a boy and now share with my family and friends.

Pan Fried Lake Trout

4 pounds skinned lake trout fillets (dolphin [fish], snapper, and snook for salt water fish)

1 cup saltine cracker crumbs

3 eggs

1/4 cup milk

1/4 teaspoon pepper

1/4 teaspoon onion powder

1/4 teaspoon garlic powder

1/4 teaspoon salt

2 cups vegetable oil

2 fresh lemons, cut into wedges

Pat fillets dry. Place saltine crumbs in a dish. Whisk eggs, milk, pepper, salt, onion powder, and garlic powder together. Dip fillets in egg mixture, then cracker crumbs. Heat oil in a heavy frying pan over high heat until smoking. Add fillets and fry for approximately 3 minutes, or until golden brown on each side (do not overcook). Drain on paper towels. Serves 8, cut recipe in half for smaller groups.

Seafood Cakes

1 pound cooked salmon or steelhead (16 ounces of canned tuna can be substituted as fish, omit directions for baking)

1/2 cup Miracle Whip dressing

1/4 cup Dijon mustard

1/4 cup finely chopped celery

1/4 cup finely chopped green onions

1/2 teaspoon salt

1/2 teaspoon pepper

1 1/4 cups dry bread crumbs

cooking oil

Bake 1 pound skinned fish fillets in covered dish at 350 degrees with a little water for 20 minutes. Let cool and flake with fork. Mix fish, dressing, mustard, vegetables, seasonings and 1/2 cup of the bread crumbs together. Shape into about 15 (2 inch) balls. Roll in the remaining 3/4 cup bread crumbs, coat well. Flatten balls into small patties. Refrigerate for 30 minutes. Heat 1/2 cup of oil in large skillet over medium-high heat. Add fish patties. Cook 5 minutes on each side or until golden brown. Makes 8 servings.

Baked Teriyaki Steaks

1 fish steak per person (such as salmon, brown trout, or any other firm fish)

teriyaki baste:

1/4 cup lite teriyaki sauce

1/3 cup green onions, chopped (include some greens)

1/8 cup honey

1 tablespoon brown sugar

1/4 tablespoon minced ginger

1 clove minced garlic

Mix all baste ingredients together. Put the fish in marinade and turn several times to coat. Cover and refrigerate several hours. Tear foil pieces to wrap the fish in. Put the marinated fish on the foil pieces and wrap tightly. Bake 350 degrees for 45-60 minutes. If desired, foil may be opened and put under broiler for a few minutes to brown. This is good served with wild rice and fresh asparagus. The sauce will do 4-6 steaks, depending upon their size.

Broiled Fish Fillets with Italian Flavor

4 fish filets (such as salmon, walleye, northern, perch, or any fairly firm fish)

Rinse with cold water and pat dry. Brush fairly liberally with Light Miracle Whip. Sprinkle with Italian style bread crumbs (approximately 1 tablespoon per filet). Cover broiler pan with foil and spray with cooking spray. Pour over desired cooking area: 1/2 tablespoon lemon juice. Lay the filets on lemon juice area and sprinkle with freshly grated parmesan cheese. Broil 6-8 inches from broiler coils for 6-8 minutes. Serve immediately.

Brown Trout Sautéed in Almond Butter

2 pounds trout filets

3/4 cup slivered almonds

1/2 stick butter

1 teaspoon lemon juice

In heavy skillet, melt butter. Add the almonds to the butter. Cook and stir until almonds turn toasted brown. Stir in the lemon juice and add the fish filets. Spoon some of the almond mix over the filets and sauté 7-10 minutes. Turn the filets and spoon more almond mixture over. Sauté another 7-10 minutes. Fish is done when it flakes easily. Place fish on a platter and spoon all of almond mixture over. Makes 4 servings.

Creole Fish Over Rice

2 pounds fresh fish that has been filleted, skinned and cut into 1-2 inch pieces. Use firm fish such as trout, walleye, northern etc.

2 tablespoons cooking oil

1 bay leaf

1 large can tomatoes, diced

2 medium onions, chopped

2 stalks celery, cut into 1/2 inch pieces

1 bell pepper, cut into 1/2 inch pieces

1 tablespoon lemon juice -- preferably fresh

In a heavy Dutch oven, heat oil. Add onion, green pepper, celery, lemon juice and bay leaf. Sauté until vegetables are tender. Remove the bay leaf and add the tomatoes. Cover and simmer for 1 hour. Add the fish pieces and simmer another 30-40 minutes or until the fish is done. Serve over cooked rice. Makes 4-6 servings.

Great Fried Fish

2 pounds (approximately) fresh brown trout fillets or any other firm fish

1/2 cup Italian style bread crumbs

1/2 cup Corn Flake crumbs

1 cup cracker meal

Mix all of above together in any size container convenient for breading the fish. Break 2 eggs in shallow container, such as a pie pan, and beat with a fork. In a heavy skillet heat 1/4 cup cooking oil and 1 stick of butter. Turn the fish several times in the egg then several times in the crumb mixture until well coated. Put the fish in the hot oil. Reduce heat to medium. (This is done so the fish will be well done all the way through, but golden brown and crisp on outside.) Cook approximately 15 minutes per side. This is very good served with seasoned french fries and cole slaw.

Grilled Salmon Steaks

Marinade:

      1/4 cup orange juice concentrate

      1 tablespoon snipped fresh chives

      2 tablespoons melted butter

      1 clove minced garlic

      1/8 teaspoon ginger

This is enough marinade for 4 salmon steaks -- approximately 2 pounds total. Mix together all ingredients of the marinade in medium size bowl. Put the steaks in and turn several times so that all is exposed. Cover and refrigerate several hours and turn several more times. Liberally spray a grill fish basket with cooking oil such as Pam. Take salmon from marinade and shake to remove excess moisture reserving marinade. Put the fish on grill over fairly hot coals. Grill for 7-8 minutes and turn. Brush with the marinade before turning. Salmon is done when it flakes easily.

Stuffed Whole Salmon on Grill

Clean the salmon, but leave skin on

2 medium onions, quartered

1 large green pepper, cut into 1 inch pieces

8-10 new potatoes, washed

2 carrots, peeled and cut into 1 inch pieces

2 stalks celery, washed and cut into 1 inch pieces

Mix 1/4 cup Italian dressing with 1 tablespoon lemon juice. Melt one stick butter and add the dressing with lemon juice. Liberally spray a piece of foil with cooking spray, such as Pam. Be sure the foil is big enough to well wrap the salmon. Stuff the fish with the vegetable pieces. Pour the butter-dressing mix over the vegetables. Wrap the fish tightly and place over medium hot grill. Put the cover on and grill for approximately 1 1/2-2 hours or until fish is well done. Makes 4-6 servings.

Fish and Sausage Paella

1 pound firm fish fillets (such as lake perch, walleye, northern, etc.)

1/2 pound smoked turkey sausage

In a large Dutch oven, sauté the following in 1/2 stick butter:

1/2 cup chopped onion

1/2 cup chopped celery

1 green pepper, cut in small pieces

Then add the smoked sausage cut into small pieces and 1 package of Spanish rice mix (without the seasoning packet). Cook while stirring for 10 minutes. Add the seasoning packet, 1 teaspoon garlic salt, 1 medium can diced tomatoes and 1 cup of hot water. Cover and simmer 20-25 minutes. Add the fish and cook 20-30 minutes longer or until the fish looks done. Makes 4 servings.

Door County Fish Boil

> 6 pounds skinned salmon or trout fillets, cut each
> fillet into 4 or 5 pieces (monk fish or cod are great
> for salt water fish)
> 3 pounds small or medium potatoes, quartered
> 2 pounds small onions
> 1/2 cup salt
> 1/2 pound margarine
> 2 tablespoons lemon juice

Fill a large pot 3/4 full of water and bring to boil. Place potatoes in a wire cooking basket. Lower basket into pot. Cook at a full rolling boil for about 3 to 4 minutes. Remove basket and add onions. Place back in pot. Add salt and continue boiling for 3 minutes. Remove basket and add fish pieces. Again lower into pot and cook 4 to 5 minutes, or until the fish and potatoes are fork tender. Melt margarine in a saucepan then add lemon juice, for a butter sauce to be served with fish. Fish can be dipped in sauce, like lobster. Serves 8 to 10. Cut this recipe in half for smaller groups, cooking time will remain about the same.

Poached Salmon with Dill Sauce

3 pounds skinned salmon fillets

1 lemon, cut into wedges

1 bay leaf

1/4 teaspoon dried tarragon, crushed

2 tablespoons margarine or butter

4 teaspoons all-purpose flour

1/2 teaspoon sugar

1/4 teaspoon dried dillweed

1 beaten egg yolk

In a fish poacher or a large roasting pan that has a wire rack with handles, add enough water to almost reach the rack. Remove and grease rack, set aside. Add 3 lemon wedges, bay leaf, tarragon, and dash salt to water. Place pan over two burners on range top. Bring to boil, then reduce heat. Lower fish on rack into pan. Simmer, covered for 35 to 40 minutes, or until fish flakes easily with a fork. Remove fish, keep warm.

Dill Sauce:

Strain cooking liquid and save 1 cup. Melt 2 tablespoons margarine or butter. Stir in 4 teaspoons all-purpose flour, 1/2 teaspoon sugar, 1/2 teaspoon dillweed, and dash salt. Add the one cup strained cooking liquid. Cook and stir until bubbly. Reduce heat and stir in 1 beaten egg yolk. Cook and stir 1 minute more. Serve sauce with fish. Serves 6. This is a gourmet dish that is usually only found in very expensive restaurants.

Capt. Ron's Canned Salmon

Wash and blot skinned salmon fillets, cut into 2 inch chunks. Pack tight in pint jars. On top of fish place:

1) 1 teaspoon salt

2) 1 teaspoon lemon juice

3) If you want pink salmon add 1 tablespoon tomato juice.

Do not add water.

Pressure cook at 15 lbs. for 90 minutes.

Smoked Salmon or Trout

5 pounds salmon or trout, fillets or steaks (mackerel, tuna, and mullet are a few good species of salt water fish for smoking)

Brine Solution--

1 gallon water

2 cups non-iodized salt

2 cups light brown sugar

Immerse fish steaks or fillets completely in brine solution for 8 hours for 1 inch thick steaks and 4 hours for fillets. Remove fish from brine. Rinse each piece with water and place on paper towels. Pat dry. In about one hour fish will have a tacky glaze, called the "pellicle." They are now ready to be loaded in the smoker (skin side down for fillets). To determine the smoking time and the amount of wood ship fuel require (apple wood is the best), refer to the instructions provided with your particular smoker. Depending on the brand and type, smoking time will vary. A good tip to give fish a sweet glazed coating and a desirable golden brown color is: put 1/2 cup of the brown sugar on the fire or fuel pan 15 minutes before taking the fish from

the smoker. My family has been smoking fish this way for
three generations.

CHAPTER *11*

HOW TO RECEIVE A VALUABLE GIFT - ABSOLUTELY FREE!

Reading through this book, you've no doubt heard me mention my boat, the "Can't Miss," out of Saugatuck Michigan, and the customers I take aboard. I've actually tried to keep it to a minimum, because I didn't want my personal feelings towards this beautiful area of Saugatuck, and my pride for my vessel and the work I do to get in the way of teaching you the finer arts of freshwater sportfishing. Now that you've completed the book, I hope you'll agree that I accomplished just that.

Plus, I hope that you use this book again and again as a reference tool for *catching more fish every time.* If you reflect back on what I have taught you so far, you'll realize that you now have the tools to be a successful fisherman every time, no matter what time of year or the location you're fishing. In other words, you'll haul in more fish than anyone on the water!

But it occurs to me that you, like most of my readers, simply want more. So I've decided to make you the following special offer. And, if you'll take just a few more minutes to read the following about fishing aboard the "Can't Miss" in the wonderful town of Saugatuck, I'll show you how to receive this very special FREE gift.

You already know that Saugatuck is situated in southwestern Michigan on the eastern shore of Lake Michigan. I've spent my entire life in this area and I can honestly say that I have never once thought about leaving. I've seen much of the United States, and I can assure you there are sights-to-see all across the country, but *nowhere* is quite like Saugatuck.

Imagine a small, sleepy midwestern town, where everyone is everyone else's neighbor. Now imagine the beautiful scenery of a winding river making its way through downtown, with miles of wooded and marshy acreage decorating its banks -- a haven for all sorts of wildlife -- literally untouched by the taint of industry so often associated with a port town. Throw in great sportfishing and maritime recreation just thirty minutes from the dock, and folks coming from all over America to enjoy the sport and the leisure. Add all of these together, and suddenly, it's not quite so sleepy anymore.

In fact, because of the quaint town with its dozens of unique little shops, the built-in recreational facilities (Lake Michigan, of course), and the friendly people, Saugatuck is one of the hottest spots for tourism in the state of Michigan. Whether you prefer the wild nightlife or a quiet day on the beach, or an exciting day on the water, or an enjoyable day of shopping, or a relaxing day of exploring the dunes, or . . . (you get the idea), Saugatuck is the perfect place for everyone and anyone.

But let me get back to my offer and that FREE gift. You see, this area is perfect for an entire family, a group of a few close friends, or just yourself to enjoy. And what better way to spend some of your free time than learning even more about freshwater sportfishing aboard the "Can't Miss" on the clean, clear, open blue water of Lake Michigan? That's right, even though I've already given you the tools necessary to catch more fish every time, my fishing expertise has come through an entire lifetime of experience

-- and that's something that could never be explained and taught in a single volume. Or if you prefer, I can recommend and book you on any number of boats with seasoned, experienced charter captains all along the coast of Lake Michigan. But before I go on, take a look at what some folks are saying about fishing aboard the "Can't Miss."

> *"Because of Captain Peel's knowledge of the lake and practical use of fishing strategies, our family's enjoyment of charter fishing 'Limits out every time!'"*
>
> *Vickie L. Seeburger*

> *"Our Reason for using 'Can't Miss' Charter Service is Mike's knowledge of the lake, where and what type of lures to use, along with his determination to catch fish. This coupled with Mike's personality means you are going to catch fish and have a great time with all kinds of stories to tell later.*
>
> *Ken Davis - Edinburgh, Indiana*

> *"Mike's knowledge of Lake Michigan and its trout and salmon is unsurpassed with any of the eight previous charter captains we have used to entertain customers."*
>
> *Drew L. Deters - Biotec, Inc.*

> *"I've spent many a summer's day fishing with Mike Peel on Lake Michigan. He is the most down to earth, hardest working charter captain I've met. No*

matter what kind of fish in the Great Lakes you want to catch, Mike can hook you up. When no one else is catching fish, Mike is!! And, when everyone is catching fish, Mike is catching MORE!!! Mike knows his business inside and out. Mike Peel, no doubt, is the best Charter Captain around."

Kim Kletzka - Livonia, Michigan

"Mike and I have fished together during April in spitting snow and cold rain, the dog days of August when there isn't a breath of wind stirring, and the clear Indian Summer weather of fall and always caught fish. There have been days when it seemed like there was a fish on one of the rods continually and we would limit out and return to the dock early. And there have been days when the fishing was slow, but never so slow that Mike could not find us a few fish. On those days when the fishing has been slow, Mike has always kept the interest of my relatives (children, grandchildren, sisters and their families), my guests and myself by telling stories about his experiences growing up in a fisherman's family.

"I remember when Mike first bought the business from his father and was the Captain with his father acting as first mate. His dad drove the boat and continued to instruct the Captain (Mike) on just how to do everything and Mike did as he was told, but slowly worked his way into the roll of Captain without his dad realizing the change was taking place. When my oldest grandson was asked recently during 'Show and Tell' at his Virginia school what he remembered best about his summer vacation, he answered without hesitation, 'Fishing on the "Can't

Miss" with Mike Peel!' This is the kind of individual Mike is, an unforgettable friend to everyone young and old who steps aboard the 'Can't Miss.' This is one of the reasons I make the trip from Tampa, Florida three of four times each year to fish with Mike for Lake Michigan salmon and trout."

John C. Norton, P.E. - Tampa, Florida

But fishing aboard the "Can't Miss" will be more than *just* an action packed, fun filled day for you. A lot more. You'll have the opportunity to experience firsthand the tips, techniques, secrets, and little known facts that turn fishing "stories" into *reality*. Plus, everyone who charters with me on the "Can't Miss," or on one of the boats I recommend and book for you, will receive a one year subscription to my comprehensive newsletter absolutely FREE! In the newsletter you will find the latest news in a changing environment, information on new products, up to the minute fishing strategies, shared secrets from successful anglers, inside insights from experts in the field, plus a whole lot more! This newsletter will truly be the most valuable fishing tool you have ever received. And, when you call to book your charter, be sure to mention that you have a copy of "How to Catch More Fish Every Time" because when you book your charter, I'll start your subscrip-

cause when you book your charter, I'll start your subscription immediately. That's my way of showing my appreciation for your business and making good my promise to you for your free gift.

But my dedication to offer supreme service doesn't stop there, either. You see, whether you fish aboard the "Can't Miss" or any boat I recommend and book you on, you will automatically be entered into my own private, exclusive, season long big fish contest. As you can imagine, I have to be the sole authority so as to resolve any discrepancies with such a contest, but if you are the lucky winner or if any member in your fishing party is the lucky winner, you will receive a FREE booking of equal value, good any time during the next season. And, all you have to do is land the largest fish of the season.

And when you catch a *trophy* fish aboard the "Can't Miss," I'll not only tell you who should mount your fish at the best possible price for the highest quality mounting job, but I'll also fill out all the paperwork necessary to assure you are recognized by the state of Michigan for your angling success!

To book a charter, simply call 616-561-2252 and speak with me personally or my wife Roxanne (don't forget to mention the book!). We would be more than happy to schedule an outing for you and your family, friends, customers, or business associates. But be prepared to have an outstanding trip! Since spaces are filling rapidly (there are only a limited number of fishable days throughout the course of a year in Michigan) call today to make your reservation. I very much look forward to meeting you personally!

GLOSSARY

ACTION OF RODS - The stiffness or taper of different models of fishing rods.

ADD-A-LINE - An extra leader and lure attached to the main line that allows you to run two lures on one down-rigger, using only one fishing pole.

ALEWIFE - A salt water bait fish which provides an excellent source of food for salmon and trout, that migrated into the Great Lakes through the St. Lawrence River system.

AMPERAGE - The amount of electric current used by or needed to operate certain electronic instruments.

ATTRACTER LURE COMBINATION - A trolling rig with an attracting device ahead of a lure to help draw a fish's attention to the lure. Some attracters also add action (movement) to the lures used with them.

BAIL - A part of a spinning reel that holds fishing line on the spool until you are ready to cast or release it.

BAIT FISH - A small fish or minnow that can be used as food by larger game fish.

BALLAST - Heavy material put into a boat or ship to provide weight and stability.

BAROMETRIC PRESSURE - Atmospheric pressure that can effect the activity and feeding patterns of fish.

BARREL SWIVEL - A swivel that has a barrel shape connector between the two eyes to which fishing lines are tied.

BASIN - A term for a specific section of a large body or area of water.

BELL SINKER - Bell refers to the shape of the sinker being narrow at the top and wide at the bottom. This shape helps it slide over obstructions without becoming snagged.

BODY BAIT - A lure which is usually made of molded plastic that has a bill or lip on it's front end to produce a swimming or vibrating action.

BOTTOM BOUNCING - Bouncing a lure or bait off the bottom of a lake or river to entice fish to strike.

BOTTOM BOUNCING - Bouncing a lure or bait off the bottom of a lake or river to entice fish to strike.

BOTTOM STRUCTURE - The composition or characteristics of the bottom of lakes, river, and streams.

BOW - The forward part of a boat.

BREAK OFF - When a fish breaks the fishing line.

BREAK - Where two different types or temperatures of water meet.

BREAKWATER - A pier head or other wall type structure designed to stop incoming waves.

BROWN TROUT - A species of trout that is usually caught in rivers and streams, or near shore in large bodies of water.

BUMPING THE BOTTOM - When a lure or weight occasionally hits the bottom while trolling.

BUOY - A floating object used to mark a desired location.

BYTHOTREPHES (B.C.) - The scientific name of the European Water Flea that was unintentionally introduced into the Great Lakes from the ballast water of foreign ships.

CANNONBALL - A spherical shaped downrigger weight.

CARCINOGEN - A cancer causing substance or agent.

CARNIVOROUS - A fish that is a flesh eating predator.

CHINOOK (King) SALMON - The largest species of salmon in North America.

CHUM - Chopped up fish or bait used to attract fish.

CHUNK SPAWN - A form of spawn that is not mature and the individual eggs are still connected by a membrane.

COCKPIT - The fishing or seating area in the upper cabin or back deck of a boat.

COHO SALMON - A species of Pacific salmon somewhat smaller than a king salmon.

COLD BLOODED - A fish or animal that's body temperature is the same as it's surrounding environment.

COWBELLS - An attracting device that is comprised of a series of spinner blades.

CRANKBAIT - A body bait (plug) that derives its action by being retrieved by a fishing reel or trolled through the water.

CRAPPIE - A species of pan fish that is found mostly in rivers and inland lakes.

CRAWFISH - A small lobster-like looking crustacean.

CRT's- Cathode Ray Tubes which are video displays used in navigation and fishing electronics.

DEEP DIVING BODY BAIT - A body bait with a large bill or lip that helps it obtain deeper depths while being retrieved or pulled through the water.

DEPTH SOUNDER - An electronic instrument used to determine the depth of water.

DIP NET - A device with a long handle and round hoop containing netting, used to land or capture fish.

DIVING DEVICES (Divers) - A device used to take lures or baits down to a desired depth while trolling without the aid of downriggers or sinkers.

DODGER - An attracting device run ahead of a lure that also adds action (movement) to the lure.

DOWNRIGGER - A mechanical device used to take baits down to a desired depth.

DRAG - The part of a reel that controls the pressure or weight that it will take to pull line out of its spool.

DRIFT - When a boat is moved or pushed by wind or current.

DROP SINKER (Drop Weight) - A method of rigging that allows a fish to release the sinker or weight from the fishing line after it is hooked.

DROP BACK FISHING - Anchoring your boat and letting the current give lures their proper action.

FAT HEAD MINNOW - An inexpensive species of minnow that is frequently used as bait for perch fishing.

FILLET - Cleaning fish in a manner that removes only the flesh from the carcass.

FINGERLING - A size description for a certain age of young game fish.

FISH FINDER - An instrument used to both locate fish and desired depth or structure of a lake or river bottom.

FLAT SINKER - A flat shaped sinker designed so that it won't roll with the current and will keep a bait in a desired location.

FLAT LINE - A fishing rod with a lure or bait that is run from a boat while trolling without the aid of a downrigger or any other trolling device.

FLOAT - A buoyant object that is used either to detect a bite or suspend a bait off the bottom while still fishing.

FLOATER RIG - A method of rigging that is used to slightly suspend baits off the bottom while still fishing.

FLORESCENT LINE - A type of line that is highly visible.

FLUKE ANCHOR - An anchor with a triangular blade that catches on the bottom easily.

FORAGE BASE - The supply of bait fish available for predatory game fish.

FOUL HOOKED - When a fish is unintentionally hooked somewhere else besides the mouth.

GAFF HOOK - A steel hook with a handle used to land large fish.

GIMBAL MOUNT - A downrigger mounting system that fits into a flush mount rod holder for easy removal.

GPS (Global Position System) - A navigation instrument that receives its data from satellites and computes this information, giving you a nearly exact present position or direction and distance of a desired destination anywhere in the world.

GRAPHITE - A material used to make fishing rods that is sensitive, light, and strong.

GUNWALE (Gunnel) - The upper edge of a boats side.

HATCHERY - A facility where fish are hatched from eggs and grown to a suitable size for releasing into a desired location.

HEAD BOAT - A charter boat that takes out large groups of passengers fishing.

IN-LINE PLANER BOARD - A small planer board that attaches directly to the fishing line itself, taking lures or baits out to the side (away from the boat) while trolling.

JIG - A lead headed lure used primarily for walleye fishing.

JIGGING - Adding action to a bait or lure by lifting and lowering the rod with a designed pattern.

KEEL WEIGHT SINKER - A sinker used for trolling with a keel built into it that gives it stability and helps reduce fishing line from twisting.

KING SALMON - A slang name for chinook salmon, the largest species of salmon in North America.

LAG - When a compass reacts slowly to a change in direction of a boat.

LCD's - Liquid Crystal Displays used in navigation and fishing electronics.

LCD's - Liquid Crystal Displays used in navigation and fishing electronics.

LEAD LENGTH - The distance a lure or bait is let out behind the boat.

LEAD CORE LINE (Lead Line) - Color coded nylon covered fishing line with the color changing every thirty feet, enabling you to determine how much line you have let out behind the boat.

LEADER - A length of line between the lure or bait and a piece of fishing equipment or attracting device.

LEVEL WIND REEL - A reel that positions the line evenly on the spool.

LORAN C - A navigation instrument that operates off radio tower signals which are picked up by a receiver and give you the present position of a boat, or the direction and distance of a desired destination.

MAIN LINE - The rod with the lure or bait attached directly to the downrigger release.

MAST - An upright pole that supports rigging of a fishing vessel.

MATURATION - To grow, mature, or develop.

MID-SHIPS - The center section of a boat half way between the bow (front) and stern (back).

MID-WATER BAIT SCHOOL - A school of bait fish that is suspended nearly mid way between the surface and bottom.

MONOFILAMENT - A type of fishing line made of a material that is small in diameter compared to it's breaking strength and is usually clear or light pigmented in color.

MOUNT - To stuff or preserve a fish to be hung on the wall or otherwise displayed.

MUDDLER - A small deep water bottom dwelling bait fish that is an excellent source of food for lake trout.

NAIL KNOT - A fishing knot used to connect lead core line to smaller diameter monofilament line.

NAVIGATION LIGHTS - Lights displayed on vessels (boats) or channel markers for navigation and safety purposes.

NIGHT CRAWLER HARNESS - A spinner lure that has a series of hooks to hold a night crawler in a straight position before the fish strikes.

NOAA - National Oceanic and Atmospheric Administration

OPEN FACE (SPINNING) REEL - A reel that is attached to the bottom of the rod (reel down) and is usually used for casting or still fishing applications.

OPTIMUM WATER TEMPERATURE - The ideal water temperature to fish for certain species.

OUTDOWN - A long arm downrigger that is positioned on the side of a boat.

OUTRIGGERS - A long fiberglass or aluminum pole that holds fishing lines out to the side of the boat while trolling.

OVER SWING - When a compass swings past the actual heading before coming back to the correct heading. (direction)

PARTY BOAT - A boat that takes out large groups of passengers to fish.

PEANUT - A type of lure that is made for use specifically behind a dodger or cowbell attracting device.

PERCH - A small fresh water food and game fish related to the walleye.

PIER HEAD - A wall type structure that protects a harbor entrance.

PLANKTON - Small organisms that young gamefish and most baitfish feed on.

PLANER BOARD - A wooden or plastic device that is used to take lures or baits out to the side (away from) the boat while trolling.

PLANT - (Stock) To put hatchery raised fish into a body of water.

PLOTTER - A navigation instrument that displays your route of travel and position.

PLUG - Another name for a body bait.

PREFERRED TEMPERATURE ZONE - The temperature at which certain species of fish prefer to feed or live in.

PREVAILING WIND - When the wind has been from a constant or persistent direction.

PULLED - To drag (troll) a lure or bait behind a moving boat.

PYRAMID SINKER - A sinker with a pyramid shape that's corners will dig into the bottom and hold it's position.

PYRAMID SINKER - A sinker with a pyramid shape that's corners will dig into the bottom and hold it's position.

RADAR - An instrument used for navigation designed to be your eyes during low visibility conditions that works by sending out a signal which is bounced off an object and returned to the unit.

REEF - An area of rock or other hard structure that raises up from the bottom, making the water shallower than the surrounding area.

RELEASE - A devise used to attach a fishing line to a downrigger or any other piece of fishing equipment that will allow the line to be pulled free after a fish hits.

RIG - 1. A type of fishing system or technique that is being used. 2. To outfit or supply equipment to a boat.

RUBBER SNUBBER - A shock absorber made of rubber tubing that is used between a diver and lure. This device helps reduce the chance of breaking the line or loosing the fish after it is hooked.

RUBBER CORE SINKER - A sinker with a rubber insert that holds it in position on a fishing line.

SALMON - A species of game and food fish that lives in open water and returns to rivers or streams to spawn.

SAND BAR - A shoal of sand deposited on the bottom of a lake or river built up by waves or current.

SCALLOP - A part of a vinyl or prism adhesive tape that is used to decorate and add color to lures.

SCUM LINE - A visible line in the water where two different types of water or currents meet that contains floating debris and or insects.

SHINER MINNOW - A shiny silver scaled minnow that is used as bait for perch fishing.

SHOAL - A shallow place in a body of water.

SINKER - A weight used for sinking a fishing line or holding a bait in place on the bottom.

SKAMANIA STEELHEAD - A strain of steelhead that spawns during the summer months.

SLICED SHANK HOOK - A fishing hook with an extra barb to hold the bait on the hook while casting or when a light bite (strike) occurs.

SLICK - A glassy or smooth appearing area on the surface of the water.

SLIP BOBBER - A bobber that is made so the fishing line can slide through it until a desired depth is obtained. At this point a stop is placed so the same depth of fishing can be repeated.

SLIP SINKER - A sinker that slides freely on a fishing line, allowing the fish to swim away with a bait without feeling resistance from the sinker.

SLIPPING - When a boat is pushed sideways by wind or current while trolling.

SMELT - A long, thin bait and food fish that is present in all the Great Lakes and some other bodies of water.

SMOLT - The age or physical condition at which a young anadromous fish will be ready to leave rivers or streams for large bodies of open water.

SNAP SWIVEL - A device used to attach a fishing line to a lure, hook, or sinker, where the swivel helps eliminate twisting of the line.

SNAP - A device used to attach a fishing line to a lure, hook, or sinker.

SNELLED HOOK - A hook with a short leader pre-tied to it.

SOUNDER - Another term for an electronic fish or depth finding instrument.

SPAWN - 1. (*n.*) Fish eggs. 2. (*v.*) When female fish lay eggs and the males fertilize them to propagate the species.

SPAWN SACK - Five to ten individual salmon or steelhead eggs placed in fine nylon netting and tied into a small cluster.

SPIN CAST REEL - A closed face spinning reel with a button to push that releases the line.

SPIN - When a compass spins unnecessarily not reflecting the actual course of the boat.

SPINNING REEL (OPEN FACE) - A reel that is attached to the bottom of the rod (reel down) and is usually used for casting or still fishing applications.

SPLIT SHOT - A small spherical shaped sinker that can be clamped on a fishing line.

SPLIT RING - A ring used to attach the hook to the lure or the fishing line to the front of the lure.

SPOON - A metal fishing lure that has a cupped shape which gives it a designed movement (action) while being pulled or retrieved through the water.

SPOON - A metal fishing lure that has a cupped shape which gives it a designed movement (action) while being pulled or retrieved through the water.

SPOT TAIL SHINER - A small bait fish that is native to the open waters of the Great Lakes. It can easily be identified by a small dark spot near its tail.

STAGING - When fish congregate near a river or stream to prepare for a spawning migration.

STEELHEAD - An anadromous species of trout native to the Pacific Northwest of North America that was introduced into the Great Lakes.

STERN - The back of a boat.

STILL FISHING - Casting out a live or dead bait and allowing the fish to come to it for the strike or bite.

STINGER HOOK - A hook that trails behind the main hook that helps catch fish that are striking short.

STOP - An object used to stop a sinker or float (bobber) from sliding past a desired point on a fishing line.

STRIKE - When a fish hits a lure or bait.

STRIPED BASS - A salt water species of bass that has been introduced to fresh water.

SURF FISHING - Fishing in an area directly out from where the water meets the shore.

SURF - An area where the waves of a body of water break on the shoreline.

SWIVEL - A device used to help eliminate twisting of fishing line.

TAPE - Adhesive tape that is put on lures to add color and attract fish.

TEST - The breaking strength of fishing line.

THERMAL BARRIER - A vertical wall of water formed when warmer in-shore waters meet colder offshore waters.

THERMOCLINE - A layer of water between the warmer surface water (epilimnion) and the colder deep water. (hypolimnion)

THREE WAY RIG - A bottom bouncing rig that uses a three way swivel where the height the bait is fished off the bottom can be regulated by the leader length to the sinker.

THREE WAY SWIVEL - A swivel with three eyes that fishing lines can be tied to.

THUMPER (Drag Anchor) - A small anchor that is used to bounce on or drag across the bottom. It is used for stirring up the bottom to attract fish, not to hold the boats position.

TRANSOM - The back (stern) of a boat.

TREBLE HOOK - A fishing hook with three points used on many spoons and body baits.

TROLLING - Using the speed of a boat to give lures proper action.

TROUT - A fresh water food and game fish related to the salmon.

VERTICAL JIGGING - Jig fishing from a boat straight down by adding action to the jig using a designed lifting and lowering pattern.

VHF RADIO - A marine band radio that has an FM frequency and is commonly used by boats or ships.

WALKING SINKER - A sinker that is designed to be dragged across the bottom without becoming snagged on obstructions.

WALLEYE - A highly sought after excellent eating fresh water game fish that is related to the perch.

WARM WATER DISCHARGE - An area where warm water that has been used to cool power plants is discharged into a large body of water.

WEIGHT FORWARD SPINNER - A spinner lure that is weighted in it's front section, that has been a traditionally used for drift fishing walleye in Lake Erie.

WIGGLER - Mayfly larvae that is used as bait for perch fishing.

WIRE BOTTOM BOUNCING RIG - A bottom bouncing rig made of a bent wire in the shape of a "V" with one leg longer than the other. The longest leg has the weight attached to it, and the shorter one the leader and bait, enabling this rig to bounce over obstructions without becoming snagged.

WIRE LINE - 1. Fishing line made of wire. 2. A rod and reel equipped with wire line used to fish deep while trolling.

CAPTAIN MIKE'S PREFERRED LURES AND EQUIPMENT CHECKLIST AND INDEX

INDEX

❧M❧

main line, 44
mast, 13-**14**
mid-water bait school, 39, 42, 55, 101, 109
muddler, 79-80

❧N❧

nail knot, **112**
navigation aides
	See also compass, Loran C, plotters, GPS, radar
netting fish, 122-124
	long handled dip net, 6
night crawler harness, 104
NOAA Weather Satellite, 59

❧O❧

open face (spinning) reel, *See* spinning reel
optimum water temperature, 19-20, **48**
	for perch, 80
outdown, 42, **43**, **46**
outriggers
	offshore spring fishing, 32-35
	fall spawning runs, 71-72
	mounting, 151-152
over swing, 136

❧P❧

party boat, 79
peanut, 54
perch
	anchoring, 83-85

&S&

salmon, *See* chinook, coho
sand bar, 11-12
scope, 90
scum line, 22-23
shiner minnow, 90
sinkers
    bell sinker, **89**
    drop sinker (drop weight), 49-51, **105**
    flat sinker, 6-7, 8
    keel weight sinker
    pyramid sinker, 6-7, 8
    rubber core sinker, 27
    sinker release, 54
    slip sinker, 27, 94, **103**
    walking sinker, 101
skamania steelhead, 68
sliced shank hook, 4
slick, 58
slip bobber, 90, 92
slip sinker, *See* sinkers
smelt, 6, 19, 80
smolt, 67
snap swivel, 4, 6, 44
snap, 44
snelled hook, **89**
sounder, *See* depth sounder
spawn/spawning
    as bait, 3-6, 8
    fall spawning runs, 65-71
    rigging, **5**
    walleye, 94-95

&**T**&

thermocline, 39-42
three way rig, 104-**105**
three way swivel, 36, 54, **105**
thumper, *See* drag anchor
tow line, **14**
transom, 144
treble hook, 4-6
trolling
    bottom fishing, 52-55
    common mistakes, 107-108
    early spring fishing, 9-12
    fall salmon, 69-70
    finding the fish, 22-23
    mid-water fishing, 47-50
    river mouths, 10-11
    T-Bar fishing, 59-61
    thermoclines, 39-41
    walleye fishing, 108-109, 113-116
    zigzag trolling, 23, 60
trout, *See* brown trout, lake trout

❧V❧
vertical jigging, 96-100
VHF radio, 21-22, 142-143

❧W❧
waders, 8
walking sinker, *See* sinkers
walleye, **93**
    bottom bouncing, 114
    jigging, 96-99, **97**

ABOUT THE AUTHOR

Michael R. Peel was born into a fishing family as a third generation fisherman. His grandfather and father were both commercial fisherman, but his father made the switch to sportfishing in the late '60s.

Capt. Peel started fishing on Lake Michigan on the commercial fishing trawler, "The Thomas C. Mullen," when he was only eleven years old. In the late '60s, along with his father, he began charter fishing for salmon and trout, and guided fisherman for northern pike on his own. Some of his other experience includes working as a first mate during the winter months in the Florida keys, several appearances on TV fishing shows, and his extensive personal pursuit of all available salt and freshwater game fish.

Since receiving his U.S.C.G. captain's license when he was 19 years old, he has been a full time captain for 23 years.

Future plans for Capt. Peel are to increase his activity as a booking agent for other boats, write more books, and continue his freelance writing for fishing magazines.